This book is dedicated to Sharla Stroup,
my wife and the love of my life.

Copyright © 2019 by John Stroup.

All rights reserved. No part of this publication may be re-produced, distributed, or transmitted in any form or by any means, including photocopying, recording, or other electronic or mechanical methods, without the prior written permission of the publisher, except in the case of brief quotations embodied in critical reviews and certain other noncommercial uses permitted by copyright law.

Some names and identifying details have been changed to protect the privacy of individuals.

Scripture quotations marked (ESV) are taken from the ESV® Bible (The Holy Bible, English Standard Version®), copyright © 2001 by Crossway, a publishing ministry of Good News Publishers. Used by permission. All rights reserved. Any **bold** or *italicized* words within Scripture quotations have been added by the author for emphasis.

Scripture quotations marked (NKJV) are taken from the New King James Version®. Copyright © 1982 by Thomas Nelson. Used by permission. All rights reserved.

ACKNOWLEDGMENTS

As I wrote this book, I couldn't help but think about all the families with whom I've come in contact—both before and after the start of Freeway Ministries. The pain, joy, victories, hardships, sleepless nights, funerals, and many unexpected events in ministering to these families have brought me to a place where I can write this book and be a tool for God's glory. I want to thank everyone who's been a part of those experiences. You are a huge component of my ministry and without God using you to impact my life, there would be no book to read or lessons to learn. To those who shared their stories, I want you to know I pray for your testimonies to impact thousands of lives. To Aaron McGuire, thank you for writing the review questions and for your counsel in my life as well as in this book. To Michelle and Tim, thank you for your investment in me and your help in writing this book.

TABLE OF CONTENTS

CHAPTER 1
Introduction — 1

CHAPTER 2
Stop Trying to Be Jesus — 7

CHAPTER 3
Stop Creating a False World — 19

CHAPTER 4
Stop Covering for Them — 35

CHAPTER 5
Stop Parenting Out of Guilt — 51

CHAPTER 6
Rock Bottom is a Great Place to Start Over — 65

CHAPTER 7
Start Investing — 79

CHAPTER 8
Start Believing—People Need Purpose — 95

CHAPTER 9
In Conclusion — 113

APPENDIX
Stop Covering for Them Testimony: Sarah's Story — 117
Stop Creating a False World Testimony: A Success Story — 125
Generational Addiction & Enablement Testimony — 131
The Sin of Addiction: Seeing Addiction as Sin and the Road to Recovery — 139

1
INTRODUCTION

There's no telling how many phone calls I get every day from people asking me if I can help their loved ones. Moms, dads, wives, husbands, pastors, and people of all kinds call to ask me to help the person they love who's fallen prey to addiction. The conversations usually start something like this: "What can I do to help my _____?" You fill in the blank. It could be a son, daughter, sibling, grandson, wife, or close friend. I listen to their story for a while, waiting for the opportunity to speak truth into their lives. Even though their stories are very different, my answer is always the same: "You have to come to a place where you realize you cannot help them." In other words, in order to truly help their loved one, they essentially have to *stop* helping—or enabling—them.

1 • INTRODUCTION

So just what is enabling? I guess that would depend on who you ask. A quick internet search gives this definition: "To give (someone or something) the authority or means to do something."[1] Enabling can be a very good thing that helps another person achieve a goal. One example would be a parent enabling a child to perform a task they couldn't do on their own, like riding a bike. By providing the bike, showing them the technique, and watching over them as they make attempts on their own, the parent has enabled the child to ride a bike. Another example would be a high school student getting a scholarship to go to college. That scholarship enables the student to work towards a degree even though they wouldn't have been able to afford college with their own resources. Enabling others to do things they *can't* do on their own is an admirable pursuit.

But enablement can be a destructive thing when it crosses over to helping people do things they *can* do on their own—an impediment that *prevents* necessary growth and change in someone's life. In the context of addiction, enabling is providing the environment in which addicts can continue their lifestyle of addiction, even though the enabler may not know that's what they're doing. They may be unwittingly

> ENABLING IS PROVIDING THE ENVIRONMENT IN WHICH ADDICTS CAN CONTINUE THEIR LIFESTYLE OF ADDICTION

---

[1] https://www.bing.com/search?q=enable&qs=n&form=QBRE&sp=-1&pq=enable&sc=8-6&sk=&cvid=39C83D34202F421782AE8B25E687AAE6.

1 • INTRODUCTION

giving a person the ability to continue to use drugs by doing things for them that they can (and should) do on their own. Without an enabler, many addicts wouldn't have the money to use drugs, the place to use them, or the vehicle to go get them. This is the type of destructive enablement I'm going to discuss in this book.

One of the problems with enablers is most of the time they are fixers by nature. Now you are thinking, *How does he know this?* Or maybe even, *What qualifies him to tell me what to do?* To be honest, I'm not a doctor, I'm not a professional counselor (though I have taken over twelve credits of counseling in college), nor do I have a degree, but what I do have is life experience. I have witnessed almost every kind of addiction and enabling situation you can imagine. I have dealt with parents, siblings, spouses, in-laws, friends, and employers of addicts, and I, myself, was strung out on drugs, homeless, and a criminal. I was given up on by society and deemed a menace. Today, by the grace of God, I am co-founder and director of Freeway Ministries and have been neck-deep in the trenches of recovery ministry for the past eight years with eleven years of my own sobriety. I invest in people's lives every day to help them overcome addiction.

My wife and I get the chance to travel through evangelism, revival ministry, programs at public and private schools, as well as equipping the church to do recovery ministry. Currently I personally oversee two men's and two women's recovery homes with the assistance of our staff. We

1 • INTRODUCTION

have three other recovery homes under our umbrella, one of them in South Africa. We have four outreaches that meet every weekend in Southern Missouri that I get to be a part of, and one in Omaha, Nebraska overseen by one of the other co-founders of Freeway. I have worked with thousands of people, countless families, children's division, law enforcement, judges, institutions, churches, schools, and many other organizations.

The model we use is very effective and by the grace of God many have been set free and are living a life they couldn't have lived before going through our program. In just the last fifteen months we have seen sixteen graduate our year-long discipleship program. These men and women are living in our recovery homes, working full-time, staying clean, active in a local church, and moving on to the next phase of their lives. Our graduates are in construction, the medical field, full-time ministry (some even pastoring churches), and all have been set free from addiction! We have worked with addicts through a proven set of principles, disciplines, tools, and the power of God to see hundreds of people set free. So, I've learned a lot about enabling and addiction, just not in a classroom. You can be assured that what I'm telling you works.

I don't want to write books just to write books. I want to write books that equip people to overcome struggles. What really made me put the pedal to the metal to write this one was a phone call I got as I was driving down the road one day.

1 • INTRODUCTION

It was a family member of an addict and she was broken. I started talking her through the issues I saw playing out in her situation. I took this loved one step-by-step through a series of questions and I could almost hear the lightbulb turning on over her head. There was a long silence, then the woman spoke in a broken voice, "Is there anything for the families of drug addicts?" Then she asked, "Mr. Stroup, do you have anything for us?" Right then my heart broke and all I could say was, "No, sorry, I don't." I knew right then I had to write this book—it is desperately needed. The person struggling with addiction is not the only person who needs help. The enabler needs it too.

> **THE PERSON ENABLING THE ADDICT ALSO NEEDS HELP**

If you're reading this, most likely someone you know is struggling with substance abuse. Maybe someone you know is an enabler and you think if you give them this book they will read it and listen to a different voice. Or you could be the person who needs to stop enabling someone you love. People who love their family members oftentimes don't know what to do to really help them and unfortunately end up making the wrong choices. I want to help change that.

My heart for this book is to help the enabler identify the problems of enablement in their own lives, assist them in breaking those unhealthy patterns, and move them forward in helping break the chains of addiction in their loved one's life. There are several real-life testimonies shared throughout

1 • INTRODUCTION

to illustrate enablement in addiction—from the pitfalls, to breaking the cycle, to the success stories—plus three in-depth testimonies in the Appendix. Each chapter ends with a *Working Through This Chapter* section which includes scenarios, instructions, and reflection questions to help you think through that chapter's concepts and how to apply them to your situation. Everything in this book finds its truth in the source of truth, and that is God's Word. I pray that you read with an open heart and gather the applicable tools to equip your family or other loved ones to battle addiction together. I am here to help you break the destructive cycle of enablement so you stop loving your kids to death.

2
STOP TRYING TO BE JESUS

2 Corinthians 12:9 (ESV)
But he said to me, "My grace is sufficient for you,
for my power is made perfect in weakness."
Therefore I will boast all the more gladly of my weaknesses,
so that the power of Christ may rest upon me.

The longest flight I've taken to date was the fifteen-hour leg from Atlanta to Johannesburg on the way to Cape Town to visit the South Africa Freeway outreach. Flying over the North Atlantic Ocean, an illustration came to me. We had a lot of turbulence and I thought, *If we go down now, we will surely die.* If a flight gets bumpy, I've learned to look to the most experienced person flying, and that person is the flight attendant. If they're calm and not panicked, I'm calm. If they look panicked, then I know we're in big trouble! But who do

2 • STOP TRYING TO BE JESUS

I want sitting in the pilot's seat when the turbulence is at an all-time high? Not a passenger, not a flight attendant, but a pilot. In this life, you are the passenger and Jesus is the pilot. You have a better chance of landing a 747 jumbo jet than doing a job only Jesus can do. The enabler is usually blind to the fact they're trying to do Jesus' job. They end up in a bad situation because they've put themselves in the pilot's seat of someone else's life.

> **JESUS IS THE PILOT & YOU'RE THE PASSENGER**

The first step in breaking the cycle of enablement in addiction is realizing you aren't Jesus. You haven't risen from the grave, you never sat down at the right hand of God, you can't convict your loved one of sin, and bottom line, you can't fix anyone. You are powerless to help someone change until they are ready to change. The sooner you realize that, the better off you and your loved one are going to be. I want you to raise your right hand and repeat after me: "From this day forward I, [your name], officially quit trying to be the governor of the universe. No longer will I try to do a job that only Jesus can do." Please listen to me and allow your loved one to come to a place where they are ready to do whatever it takes to overcome their addiction. The only way they will ever get there is if you step back and allow them to be broken. You cannot do this for them because you're not Jesus.

The Scripture at the beginning of this chapter is a good one to memorize for times of pain and suffering, and there is nothing more painful than watching someone destroy their

2 • STOP TRYING TO BE JESUS

life through addiction. Addiction is just as painful—if not more so—for those who love the addict. The person consumed by addiction is numb under the power of drugs or alcohol, but the family isn't numb. The addict doesn't feel the same pain the loved one feels. I am sorry for your pain and I write this with a pastor's heart: you will not fully allow God's power into your situation until you realize how helpless you are to change it. You are helpless on your own, but God is all-powerful. His power is made perfect in your weakness.

GOD'S POWER IS MADE PERFECT IN YOUR WEAKNESS

There are many biblical illustrations of people being changed through a radical conversion, and that is what it took for me. However, I also know hundreds of people who came to Christ as a child who never had to go through the difficult things I went through. To me that is a powerful testimony because they were kept from that life of sin by the grace of God. For many, though, it takes hardship, struggling, loneliness, and losing everything to come to a place of brokenness to seek Christ's salvation.

Let's look at one of these radical conversions through the lens of the Bible. Genesis 25 introduces us to Jacob, a momma's boy in the middle of a family battle. Jacob stayed close to home and, in my opinion, was babied by his mother. Even though the Bible doesn't say that word-for-word, you can read between the lines. The name Jacob basically means "manipulator," and every addict I meet is a Jacob while in addiction. Jacob was in cahoots with his mother—deceiving his father and manipulating his older brother, Esau—to hustle the first-born blessing so he would get the larger portion of the inheritance (see Genesis 27). He ended up on the run because his big brother promised to kill him in revenge once his father passed away. With fear in his heart, away from his home and enabling mother for the first time, Jacob and his situation began to change. Why? He changed because he had to man up and face life on his own.

Imagine the scenario for a moment. In Genesis 28:11, Jacob is far away from home and literally has a rock for a pillow. I wonder what went through his mind. It was dark, he was alone, and most likely terrified of his brother finding him. This is the lonely place where he meets with God and makes a commitment to Him (see Genesis 28:18-22). Later when he's a family man and a hard worker, God calls him on his commitment (see Genesis 31). As he is traveling to his old neighborhood, he begins to revert back to his old way of thinking because of his past sins. In fearing his brother's wrath, he starts manipulating the situation instead of trusting God to protect him. Jacob is afraid, and rightly so, but in his fear of Esau he starts hustling again. Jacob's goal is to sweet-talk his brother with flattery (Genesis 32:4) and gifts (Genesis 32:5, 17-20). After sending his family ahead of him over the brook, he finds himself all alone (Genesis 32:22-23). What happens to Jacob when he is all alone facing his past? Someone grabs him out of nowhere and Jacob begins the

2 • STOP TRYING TO BE JESUS

wrestling match of his life. Who do you think Jacob thought he was wrestling with? I believe he thought it was Esau or one of his soldiers, seeing as there were 400 men with him. But it wasn't his brother or one of his brother's men—it was God, Himself.

You may be asking, *What does this have to do with this chapter?* Please don't miss the point I'm trying to make. Jacob had to wrestle with God

> **JACOB HAD TO WRESTLE WITH GOD ALL ALONE**

all alone—no one else could be there to help him. Jacob wrestled with God all night and this had to happen for Jacob to become the man God called him to be. Please save your place, pick up a Bible, and take the time to read Genesis 32. Really study the verses where Jacob wrestled with God (24-32). God asked Jacob what his name was while they were wrestling. Studying this passage, I asked myself, *Why did God ask Jacob this question?* I believe God was seeing if Jacob would admit who he was, reminding Jacob of his sin of pretending he was Esau to get the first-born blessing. Jacob admitted who he was, and then asked God a question: "What is your name?"

Now consider the situation at hand. Jacob was wrestling with a man in the dark wishing someone would rescue him, but he was alone and had to face the situation by himself. As far as Jacob was concerned, his life was about to end. His family would be without a father, his wives would be without their husband, and all hope would be gone. During what seemed to be the worst situation imaginable,

2 • STOP TRYING TO BE JESUS

Jacob sensed something divine happening. The Bible reads that Jacob's hip was taken out of socket. That's just mentioned like it's no big deal. Why does the Bible say this? Think for a moment of the pain Jacob went through. The most common cause for a hip dislocation is a car crash, and according to orthopedic doctors it would take a powerful collision for something like this to happen.[1] Yep, Jacob was in a head-on collision with God. It was just Jacob and God alone. That is exactly what needed to happen to Jacob, and that is what needs to happen in your loved one's life. Jacob had to meet this God who was pursuing him with blessings and promises. He had to meet him alone, without his mom, dad, wife, or anyone else around. It was just Jacob and God in a dark and scary place.

Before we leave this example, I want to highlight a very important point a lot of people miss. Jacob asked God a question during his wrestling match. Now be mindful this was not a short scrimmage, but a fight for control that went on all night long until the sun was coming up (Genesis 32:26). Jacob asked the Lord, "What is your name?" and God replies, "Why do you ask me my name?" I love mysteries like this in God's Word when it doesn't explain why something happens or what something means. In my personal opinion, God was saying to Jacob, "Why are you asking me my name? Don't you recognize me?" Jacob knew who He was because after the wrestling match he named the place *Peniel*, which means "the

---

[1] https://orthoinfo.aaos.org/en/diseases--conditions/hip-dislocation.

face of God" (Genesis 32:30). Throughout his life, Jacob was wrestling with someone—whether it was his brother, his dad, his wife, or his uncle—but the real wrestling match was with God. He had manipulated others his whole life to get the blessing that had already been promised to him before he was even born (see Genesis 25:23). The blessing of God comes through surrender and humility rather than manipulation and acting in our own strength. It's a shame we have to go through so much to get to that place.

> **GOD'S BLESSING COMES THROUGH SURRENDER & HUMILITY, NOT MANIPULATION & OUR OWN STRENGTH**

I speak from experience when I say that. My mother was my best friend and she tried her best to raise me. Even though we were poor, she enabled me. She gave me everything I wanted even if she had to steal it. She thought this was what a good mom should do. I was a spoiled brat and thought the world owed me something. It was in a prison cell after being homeless and strung out on the needle, friendless with no one to visit me, and facing a world of rejection that I had my own wrestling match with God. I can give many examples of people I've met through my personal experience in ministry who have a story like this too. It wasn't until they were alone, cold, and hungry that they surrendered.

What would have happened to Jacob if his mother or someone else tried to help him during his wrestling match?

2 • STOP TRYING TO BE JESUS

Jacob had to do it on his own. He had to surrender and come to the place where he wrestled with God—just Jacob and God alone. This is exactly where your loved one needs to be. Stop trying to be Jesus and allow your loved one to come to that place of surrender.

2 • STOP TRYING TO BE JESUS

WORKING THROUGH THIS CHAPTER

IDENTIFYING THE PROBLEM

As sinful people we try to do a job that only God can do. The enabler cannot wrestle with God for their Jacob. You can pray for them and witness to them, but you cannot do the work for them. When you do the work for them, you're hindering them. You cannot change anyone, so quit trying. Your motivation is not their motivation—this is not your wrestling match. Stop trying to be Jesus.

BREAKING THE PATTERN

Before you try to help, make sure you're not trying to do a job that isn't yours to do. Ask yourself, *Am I helping or hurting?* For example, if you know your loved one is buying drugs, what happens if you give them money? Well, you just supported their drug dealer and possibly gave them what they needed to overdose. Also ask yourself:

- Am I attempting to do a job that only God can do?
- Am I trying to convict them of sin?
- Am I trying to make decisions for them?
- Am I doing something for them that they should do for themselves?

2 • STOP TRYING TO BE JESUS

Remind yourself that you're not Jesus, and make sure you're not trying to do a God-sized job in your loved one's life. There is nothing wrong with encouragement or advice but make them do the work. Sometimes drawing the line between helping and hurting is hard to do. Here are some examples of ways to help without enabling. I'll discuss this in more detail in Chapter 7, "Start Investing."

- Meet your loved one for a burger and pray with them. Give them resources to read and let them know you're not giving up on them.
- Share Scripture with them—God's Word is the most powerful thing you have on your side. I would argue the Bible is the best book for recovery, period. Through God's Word I was set free.
- Find out where there are meetings your loved one can be ministered to and connect them with the leadership of those meetings. Don't be afraid to go with them—your loved one will be more likely to go if you go with them, and you need help just as much as they do!

2 • STOP TRYING TO BE JESUS

 **MOVING FORWARD**

Study the story of Jacob and remind yourself of its truths when you are tempted to enable. I know this sounds a bit out there, but preach to yourself. No one talks to you more than you do, so preach Scripture to yourself when you're tempted. Tell yourself, *My [loved one's name] has to wrestle with God on their own. I cannot jump in this fight for them!* Remind yourself that brokenness—more often than not—comes from being alone, afraid, and in a desperate place. I am in no way telling you to abandon your loved one, but I am telling you to make sure your actions don't enable them.

2 • STOP TRYING TO BE JESUS

❓ REFLECTION QUESTIONS

Answer these questions in a notebook to help you think about and apply the concepts in this chapter.

1. What is the current situation you're going through trying to help someone?
2. What do you fear is going to happen if you stop helping them?
3. What is your motive or purpose for helping them?
4. How are you trying to land the plane when only God can?
5. How are you keeping the person you love from wrestling with God alone like Jacob did?
6. In what ways can you help but not enable?
7. Please take time to examine your own life to make sure you are clean, holy, and pure so you may do the Father's will when seeking to help others.

3

STOP CREATING A FALSE WORLD

Proverbs 30:24-28 (ESV)
Four things on earth are small, but they are exceedingly wise:
the ants are a people not strong, yet they provide their food in the summer;
the rock badgers are a people not mighty, yet they make their homes in the cliffs;
the locusts have no king, yet all of them march in rank;
the lizard you can take in your hands, yet it is in kings' palaces.

Proverbs 6:6-9 (ESV)
Go to the ant, O sluggard; consider her ways, and be wise.
Without having any chief, officer, or ruler, she prepares
her bread in summer and gathers her food in harvest.
How long will you lie there, O sluggard?
When will you arise from your sleep?

When I study the book of Proverbs, I marvel at its truths. Written centuries ago, its simple principles are still highly relevant today. According to Tremper Longman,

3 • STOP CREATING A FALSE WORLD

Proverbs highlights two kinds of wisdom: intellectual and emotional.[1] Intellectual wisdom is the type of wisdom that helps a person solve math problems or get a 100% in English 2 in college (one of the hardest classes I've taken). Emotional wisdom is totally different; it helps a person solve daily problems and journey through life. Think about this for a second. Solomon, said to be the wisest man of his time, used four creatures to illustrate wisdom in the book of Proverbs. He could have used anything he wanted and chose four things that have no intellectual wisdom, yet are "exceedingly wise." What do these little creatures possess that would make Solomon call them out as models of wisdom? Simply put, their ability to navigate through life.

Reading Proverbs makes me reflect on our society, the state of our communities, and those who are struggling with addiction. The wisdom that comes from God and the wisdom to help a struggling addict is the same kind of wisdom used by the ant, rock badger, locust, and lizard. These four things are exceedingly wise because they possess the ability to navigate their life. Stop and ask yourself, "Am I helping _____ learn how to navigate their life?" Think about your answer for a moment. Most times, this is exactly what the enabler desperately wants for the person fighting addiction, but

> **AM I HELPING MY LOVED ONE LEARN HOW TO NAVIGATE THEIR LIFE?**

---

[1] Longman, Tremper. *How to Read Proverbs*. InterVarsity Press, Downers Grove, IL. 2002.

3 • STOP CREATING A FALSE WORLD

enabling them is not the answer because it prevents them from learning how to navigate their world on their own. Whenever you enable someone, you are creating a world for them that doesn't actually exist—a world in which someone else is helping them do the things they need to do on their own in order to successfully navigate their life. Stop creating a false world for them because you're doing more harm than good.

> **ENABLING CREATES A FALSE WORLD FOR THE ADDICT**

There are two worlds in every addict's life: the real world and the false world of addiction. They're both "real" to the addict, but one is a false world that requires a different worldview in order for it to exist. I'm thinking of the people I see holding up those signs every day as I drive to work. Please don't think I'm not heavy-hearted about homelessness, because that is not the case. I work with homeless people on a regular basis and I'm not putting them all in the same boat, but many of them live in a false reality that is much like the one created by an enabler. In other words, these people can only exist in this false world if someone enables them to. In this false world, they don't have to get up at a certain time, work, clean their room, follow any structure, or submit to authority and someone else pays their way through life once their monthly government check is gone. Most of us live in the real world and the addict needs to as well in order for their life to change. This change will happen when the false world of enablement goes away.

3 • STOP CREATING A FALSE WORLD

The person being enabled is much like that person holding the sign who survives panhandling on the busy intersection I drive past every day. The sign says, "WILLING TO WORK," but if you stop and say, "Hop in the truck. I have a full day's work for you," you will find that 95% of the time the sign says something else altogether. That sign really says, "ENABLE ME." Think about the world the enabler is creating for the addict: a world where you don't have to work to eat; a world where someone else does everything for you; a world where everything is handed to you; a world where authority doesn't matter. This is the false world the enabler creates for the addict. The longer you wait on them hand and foot, the longer you are crippling them. In the real world you have to work to earn money. Then you have to use that money to purchase food and pay your bills. If I don't buy food, my fridge is empty…but not the one being enabled—food just magically appears in their fridge!

But what happens to this person's world once the enabler passes away? Can the person you're enabling make it through life without you? When the real world hits them head-on, they're in trouble. One of the goals I have for my kids is that they're able to make it in the real world when I'm no longer here. The real world is waiting for your son, daughter, grandchild, or friend and that world is nothing like the false world created through enablement. I am someone who can speak from experience on this point. My mother enabled me my whole life. In saying this, I by no means want to disrespect her in any way. She did the best she could and I'm forever grateful for the love she had for me. I think about her every day and wish I could've turned my life around before she passed away so she could've seen what God has done, but that isn't how things went. When she passed, I was a disrespectful twenty-year-old punk who couldn't care less about authority and felt like the world owed me something. I was hurting, missing my mother, and out in the world with no understanding of how to grieve in a healthy way. I also didn't have any idea how to navigate the real world I was suddenly forced to be in.

    I want you to think about someone you know who is enabled. That person is most likely living with an unrealistic worldview. They feel like everyone owes them something, and this something is coming to them for nothing. They can sleep all day yet the house is kept clean and the laundry is done. They can dirty the dishes and someone else does them. It's almost like they have a butler who is paid with an ungrateful attitude. This person is always looking for work, but no one is ever hiring. Whenever they do get a job it is short-lived and it's always someone else's fault they got fired. Correcting this entitlement attitude is one of the purposes of our discipleship houses. I tell our guys and gals all the time, "We're not your momma." They are held accountable for their bills, behavior, tidiness, attitude, timeliness, character, integrity, language, and so on.

PEOPLE BEING ENABLED OFTEN HAVE AN ATTITUDE OF ENTITLEMENT

3 • STOP CREATING A FALSE WORLD

Many times I have to tell families to stop giving money to their loved ones living in our program. I also tell them to stop coming to see them so much. I cannot help but think of a man we'll call Grandpa Tom. His grandson was placed in our program and would run his grandpa ragged. Grandpa Tom would take him to work, take him lunch, pick him up, run him to cash his check, and so on. I explained to Tom that he needed to back off because it was having a negative effect on this young man's recovery. This young fella didn't have to do a thing for himself because his grandpa was like a part-time butler and personal chauffer all wrapped up in one. While the other men in the house were getting up early to walk to the bus, this young man was just calling grandpa to come to his rescue. Tom didn't understand why I wanted to make him walk to the bus stop and wait outside when he was happy to pick him up. He didn't understand why I would want him to be inconvenienced by the long bus route around the city when he could take him straight to his destination. He would ask, "Why would you want him to take an extra hour or two when I'm willing to take him where he needs to go?" My answer to Grandpa Tom was something Warren Wiersbe said: "The bumps are what you climb on."[2]

The grandson put himself in this position through his past actions and his grandpa was hindering him from feeling any of the "bumps" and learning how to climb up them on

---

[2] Wiersbe, Warren W. *The Bumps Are What You Climb On: Encouragement for Difficult Days*. Baker Books, Grand Rapids, MI. 2016.

3 • STOP CREATING A FALSE WORLD

his own. You can't build muscle without resistance—climbing makes a person strong. I've had people in the program whose parents did everything for them  and it ruined their recovery. Sometimes a client will enter the program and mom or dad will have a car ready for them. I won't let them have it but make them ride the bus instead. They need to be humble and grateful and see how much God can do with them if they will apply the truth found in God's Word to their lives. But this humble gratitude doesn't come from them living in the false world of enablement. When they enter our program, we direct them to get on that bus to look for work. Once they really apply themselves and find a job, they are changed. They realize they can do this without mom and dad's help.

I think about the long trips I took through the city on that bus my first year out of prison. I will never forget how hard it was, but I am thankful for that season of my life. Today, ten years later, I drive through the city on those same streets, past those busses and, from time to time, even down the alley to the homeless shelter I stayed at. Many times I have my eleven-year-old son with me and will tell him the story of where his daddy came from. It was nothing short of hard work and effort. I would not be who I am today without it and the men and women in our discipleship houses have to do the same. It builds up their confidence in what is possible without someone else doing everything for them. There is something about depending on yourself, facing rejection, struggling, busting your hind-end, and then getting that first full paycheck that changes a person's attitude. They are learning to survive without their mom, dad, aunt, uncle, grandpa, or whoever doing everything for them. That is the key to this chapter. Don't you want to see them make it in life without you? What happens when you're not around to bail them out? Hey, friend, that city bus will be there to give them a ride long after you pass away!

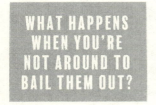

I want to share a story of a woman who was so co-dependent she couldn't do anything without her husband's help. We'll call her Sam. Sam came to Freeway from a local treatment center and was married to a man who was also a severe drug addict. They lost their kids and she had a restraining order on him. When she entered the discipleship house she acted like a wounded bunny rabbit. She was so used to him doing everything for her that she couldn't even think on her own. Monday morning came and she needed to get on the bus to look for work, because that's what people in our program do if they don't have a job. Now, I understand people can do most everything online these days, but there is something about getting out there that's needed for the addict. They can go to a career center or a library and use their computers—they just have to get out there on their own and do it.

That Monday morning we received a call from the women's house leader, Hannah. She told my wife, Sharla, that

3 • STOP CREATING A FALSE WORLD

Sam was having a panic attack because she didn't think she could go look for a job all by herself. She lacked the confidence to walk to the bus stop, wait for the bus, and travel through the city on her own. I understand this can seem overwhelmingly difficult to some. I get it, but it's necessary for the person who's been enabled. Sam literally balled up in a corner and wept like a baby because she was afraid she couldn't accomplish this task by herself. Hannah happened to have the day off and went with Sam to the bus stop then walked her through the rest of it. They had a great time and made a day out of it. Sam ended up enjoying what she thought she couldn't do alone. Imagine for a moment the confidence she gained that day.

Oh, it gets so much better! Sam became a pro at the bus and discovered she was also a very hard worker. When she got a job as a housekeeper at a local hotel she excelled at it and gained so much confidence from the hard work. She had no idea what it was like to do things on her own. Sam was climbing on those bumps. She not only was a good employee, but she became the first maintenance woman for the hotel. She was trusted with keys, got a raise, and began the journey to get her kids back from the state. Sam needed to struggle, be afraid, face the new challenges ahead of her, and overcome them. She did it herself—no one had to do it for her. How awesome is that? We were helpless to change her, but she was willing to do the work herself. Welcome to the real world, Sam! Her story is an illustration of the wisdom found in the book of Proverbs. The wisdom allowing the ant, rock

3 • STOP CREATING A FALSE WORLD

badger, locust, and lizard to navigate life on their own is the same wisdom we teach our men and women. It's the same wisdom the enabler *prevents* their loved one from gaining when they create a false world through enablement. Stop creating this false world for your loved ones!

3 • STOP CREATING A FALSE WORLD

WORKING THROUGH THIS CHAPTER

IDENTIFYING THE PROBLEM

The false world created through enablement hinders a person from growing up and learning how to live on their own. Some of you have purchased this book for an enabling family member who won't listen to you. Others were given this book as a gift because they're loving someone to death as we speak and need help. If you are the enabler, you have to recognize you're actually harming the person you love and stunting them from growing into an adult by creating this false world. You love them and want to help them but you're ultimately helpless to do so, remember? You cannot change them, but you can stop creating a false world for them. Allow them to fall down, get back up, and learn to navigate life on their own.

BREAKING THE PATTERN

I want you to ask yourself this question: "Am I creating a false reality for my loved one?" If so, do you want them to wake up to the real world? Then practice what you are learning in this book. Don't participate in crippling them by allowing them to live in a world of enablement. You don't want to create a sign holder out of your son or daughter! <u>God can reach down into their heart to do this, but He is hindered</u>

3 • STOP CREATING A FALSE WORLD

<u>by those who continue to cushion their fall.</u> Think about it. You want your family member to be able to survive on their own without you, because one day you won't be there to take care of them.

Many reading this book are filled with guilt because of past mistakes in parenting. You messed up as a parent and now you're trying to make up for it by creating a false world for your children or grandchildren through enablement. If this is you, please see Chapter 5, "Stop Parenting Out of Guilt" for more help.

It only takes one mom to enable their child and then enable her grandchildren from that child to cripple two generations. I have seen this in ministry. As I write, I am thinking of a young man who entered our program who went back to his hometown to live with his grandmother because Freeway was too hard for him. She had also enabled this young man's dad who has been in

IT ONLY TAKES ONE ENABLER TO CRIPPLE MULTIPLE GENERATIONS

and out of prison his whole life. She also enabled his brother who is in prison with this young man's dad. Right now this grandmother is allowing the young man to live with her and it's just a matter of time before he's back on drugs. Here's the honest truth that will make some shut this book, but for some it may make the light come on: the only way these men will change is if the grandmother dies or stops allowing them to come live at her house. Now her grandchildren have children.

3 • STOP CREATING A FALSE WORLD

What about them? The cycle will continue unless she stops enabling. This grandmother needs help just as much as they do. Please see the Appendix for another testimony about generational addiction and enablement.

How long will you wait before you put your foot down and make the addict wake up to reality? Here are some steps to take.

- Look to the Scripture at the beginning of this chapter. Pray for that kind of wisdom in the life of the person you love who is struggling with addiction.
- Quit paying their bills, take away the car you're paying for, and stop being a free childcare service. You're a parent, not a butler.
- Create a way to help that makes them do the work. For example, get them a week's worth of bus passes and take them to the bus stop.
- If they're living with you, give them a date to move out and stick to it. Many times the enabler gets fed up and makes a threat, but it's just that—a threat to add to the many others they've made. This time give them a date and put it on the calendar. If you have to go to the police station or call law enforcement to get them out, do it.
- Find a program somewhere they can move into and don't be afraid to look out of state.
- Start going to recovery classes yourself and get involved in a faith-based meeting of some kind. Do you know that faith-based meetings are full of people who can help you?

3 • STOP CREATING A FALSE WORLD

There are moms, dads, grandparents, and others who would love to help you walk through this battle.

 **MOVING FORWARD**

For some, it's now a waiting process and your job is to pray for the person in addiction. You evicted them from your home, you stopped giving them money, you're not being their chauffer or butler, and now you haven't heard from them. You know that they're using and you're worried about them. This is a hard spot to be in. Even though you have been blamed, name called, guilted, and labeled a hypocrite, it's not your fault. Sometimes people who are doing the right thing—like you—just need to be told you're doing a good job. If you're following the instructions I'm giving you and things seem to be getting worse, just remember that sometimes things need to get worse before they get better.

3 • STOP CREATING A FALSE WORLD

REFLECTION QUESTIONS

Answer these questions in a notebook to help you think about and apply the concepts in this chapter.

1. What is the difference between emotional wisdom and intellectual wisdom?
2. What are the instructions your loved one isn't following?
3. In what ways are you blinding the person to reality, creating a false world?
4. What empty promises has the person in need made? How have you responded to those promises?
5. What accountability are you requiring of your loved one? What accountability are you not requiring?
6. How are you preventing the person in need from climbing up those bumps of success?
7. What causes you to not have faith in God's way of healing your loved one?

4
STOP COVERING FOR THEM

Proverbs 28:13 (ESV)
Whoever conceals his transgressions will not prosper,
but he who confesses and forsakes them will obtain mercy.

Proverbs 11:14 (ESV)
Where there is no guidance, a people falls,
but in an abundance of counselors there is safety.

Proverbs 15:22 (ESV)
Without counsel plans fail,
but with many advisers they succeed.

Someone once said, "A secret is something you tell one person at a time." I like that quote. I don't like it because I enjoy good gossip, but because it's so true. One thing I've learned from being in the trenches of recovery ministry is that some things just need to be told. Now, there is a serious call to discernment here, and one should be very careful how they handle a matter. Of course I would never tell someone to broadcast another person's sin across social media or something of that nature. Your loved one is someone you care about dearly. The closer they are to you, the harder it is to expose their sin, but there comes a time in a person's addiction when their loved ones need to call in the troops. This is not a first resort by any means, but it needs to happen if the addict refuses to seek and accept help.

I reflect on Matthew 18:15-17 where Jesus begins a discourse on church discipline. He is talking to his disciples about how to handle someone who is sinning against them. He speaks of confronting that person one-on-one. Scary, huh? Then, if that doesn't work, they are to bring one or two more into the situation. If the person still refuses to listen, you're to bring the church into the situation. You may be thinking, *This is not a brother sinning against me, but my wife [or husband, son, mother, father, or _____] in a sinful situation.* These procedures are applicable to any relationship or sin situation.

EXPOSING SIN THAT'S HARMING A LOVED ONE IS PART OF LOVING THEM

Biblically we are called into relationship with each other and exposing their sin is the right thing to do. We are called to love each other and part of that is exposing sin that is harmful to those we love. Ephesians 5:8-17 teaches us to find out what is acceptable to the Lord, then do it—to expose sin and not take part in it. Covering for a loved one is never okay. We need to gently confront the person then wait on them to respond. Wisdom is required in the amount of time a person waits between talks with your loved one. Jesus doesn't say, "Confront them and wait a day for them to respond." He doesn't give us a timeframe to involve another person either. We must have discernment in this—praying for wisdom is crucial. "If any of you lacks wisdom, let him ask God, who gives generously to all without reproach, and it will be given him" (James 1:5, ESV).

Right now you may be neck-deep in covering for your wife or your husband. Maybe it's your brother and your parents have no clue what's going on. You're thinking, *My _____ would never forgive me if I told _____ what was happening.* You know that telling someone about your loved one's addiction would make them furious. Your loved one trusts you to keep their secret and when you tell they may never talk to you again. They may have already threatened you with, "I will never forgive you if you ever tell _____!" Maybe it's grandpa, dad, uncle Jim, a son, a family friend, a pastor, a Sunday school teacher, their boss, or a big brother/sister. Why do you think being exposed to a certain person or people is so scary to them? It's because of the level of respect they have for that person and the consequences they'll face.

We all need accountability in our life. My good friend, Kenny Hale, told me, "John, rules keep an honest man honest." This was part of a conversation concerning me being

4 • STOP COVERING FOR THEM

accountable as I direct Freeway Ministries. I am thankful to be surrounded by godly people I respect who not only invest in, encourage, and sharpen, but also challenge me. They hold me accountable, check on me, and sometimes let me know in a graceful way that my idea may not be as good as I thought it was. This has happened many times and I'm so grateful to have these kinds of people in my life. The addict also needs this kind of accountability. So, if they still won't stop after being confronted, you must call in the troops—the addict needs to be exposed as soon as possible. Despite their threats, at some point they will forgive you, and in the end the family will be grateful for your courage as well.

> RULES KEEP AN HONEST MAN HONEST

When my mother was sick with emphysema, she was on an oxygen hose that came out of a machine that stayed plugged into the house. It was a long hose that would go from the living room all over the house—into her bedroom, the bathroom, and kitchen. She couldn't leave the house because the portable tank wasn't strong enough. She was in bad shape and I knew it. I have three brothers and two sisters I know of, all of whom have different fathers and are way older than me. It was always my mom and me as long as I can remember due to the age gap between my siblings and me. So, my mother and I were very close. Not only was my mother my best friend, but she was my crime partner as well. One of my brothers lived close by and would stop in and check on mom, but my sisters lived far away in Illinois. One day she looked at me and said, "John, if your sisters call and ask how I'm doing, you better not tell them how sick I am. I just want to be left alone." I remember saying, "Mom, they're worried about you. What am I supposed to tell them when they call and want to talk?" I was a teenage boy and didn't want to betray my mom. "Tell them I have my days and nights mixed up." So, I lied to them.

Mom got really bad. The fluid from her lungs began to fill her tear ducts. Her eyes were swollen shut and she was dying in her bedroom. I knew I had to tell my sisters. They were calling every day, asking to speak to mom. Eventually I told them the truth and they came from Illinois to see her. Mom was so mad. My sisters called an ambulance and then my mother had a heart attack. She was taken to the hospital and never made it out. My sisters and other family members spent time with my mom through this. They did all they could to help her, but in the end she passed away.

What would have happened if I wouldn't have told my sisters about my mother's situation? How do you think they would have felt knowing that I'd been covering for my mom and lying to them? I want to be as transparent as I can with you. I still have a great amount of guilt about this situation, a guilt that may never totally go away. My mother had a terminal illness, not a drug addiction, but there are a lot of similarities. Think about it for a minute. What happens if that person dies and you knew the whole time how sick in addiction they were and yet you withheld that information?

4 • STOP COVERING FOR THEM

The guilt, shame, and burden from a situation like that leaves a person with a heavy load to carry for the rest of their life. Exposing your loved one to those who love them is exactly what you need to do. Follow Matthew 18:15-17 and use the tools Jesus gave us in Scripture.

Maybe it's a father who would rather die than have his son find out about his addiction. Maybe your loved one is a functioning addict with an excellent career and the worst thing that could happen is for the boss to discover what's going on. What I have found, though, is that those people finding out oftentimes is the very thing leading to freedom from addiction. The boss finds out and tells him, "It's rehab or you're fired." The son finds out and says, "If you ever want to see your grandchildren again you have to get help." This is part of rock bottom and even though it doesn't feel good, it is much needed. Yes, it is scary, painful, and stressful to the person who is exposing the addict, but it's necessary.

Think for a moment about how God operates. He operates in the light and the enemy operates in the dark. Light and darkness are also metaphors for one's spiritual condition. Light corresponds with honesty, integrity, transparency, accountability, and fellowship. Darkness is a picture of dishonesty, lack of integrity, secrecy, no accountability, and no fellowship. There's a huge contrast between light and darkness. Whenever you cover for your

> **GOD OPERATES IN LIGHT & THE ENEMY OPERATES IN DARKNESS**

4 • STOP COVERING FOR THEM

loved one, you're helping them stay in the dark. I know that everyone who reads this book may not see the world through a biblical worldview, but as a Christian we should. Part of the problem is that we stop looking at the world through God's Word and begin to water it down with the world's opinion. Let's take a look at addiction from a biblical worldview using what the Apostle John writes about hiding sin versus exposing it in 1 John 1.

1 John 1:5-7 (ESV)
This is the message we have heard from him and proclaim to you, that God is light, and in him is no darkness at all. If we say we have fellowship with him while we walk in darkness, we lie and do not practice the truth. But if we walk in the light, as he is in the light, we have fellowship with one another, and the blood of Jesus his Son cleanses us from all sin.

I want to share one of the most life-changing moments of my ministry. I received a message for help through the Freeway Ministries website from a woman named Sarah. When I called her number I heard the broken voice of a scared wife. She explained that her husband, Hank, was waking her up in the middle of the night and seemed deranged. Sarah was a very faithful wife, a devoted Christian, and loyal to her husband. I told her, "You are in danger and need to leave as soon as you can." I'm not going to go into all the details of Sarah's situation, but in my opinion she was too loyal to her husband and refused to leave him even though she wasn't safe. I told her she wasn't ready for my help, and to call me back when she was willing to do whatever it takes. She called a few weeks later. I talked her through packing her bags and

4 • STOP COVERING FOR THEM

literally step-by-step out the door. She was crying as I was instructing her. "Are you walking outside?" I asked. In a broken voice she replied, "Yes, I'm walking out the door." Then I said, "Get into the car and drive. Are you driving?" She said, "Yes, I'm leaving the house." Then I told her to drive to a hotel at least an hour away and tell the front desk she wanted to remain anonymous.

Once she was in that hotel room, I told her to call in the troops. The troops are people Hank loved and respected—people who also loved and respected him, wanted the best for him, and wouldn't gossip. She was to call and tell them to come to the hotel room and that it was an emergency, but not to tell her husband. Once everyone was there she told them everything. Now Sarah had a team to help. The next day Hank called me demanding to know why I told his wife of over thirty years to leave him. Hank was hot, and honestly I thought this might be the situation that ended my life. Things got hairy for all of us, including Sarah, her children, and Hank. But in the end it worked out better than we could have expected. This is what Sarah had to say about covering for Hank.

> "THE TROOPS": PEOPLE THE ADDICT LOVES & RESPECTS WHO WANT THE BEST FOR THE ADDICT

> *Once I stopped covering, it was out! I now had tons of people praying for our situation who had no idea they needed to pray for us before as a direct result of me hiding*

"the secret." I now had help and support where pride had kept me from having any support or help for many years. I now had a plan of action that I never knew existed instead of just wondering what to do and trying to control it myself. I had searched high and low for secret help and support but I was isolated by both secrecy and my actual location. Once the secret was out, the ball was rolling and it was in the Lord's mighty and capable hands. I was FINALLY out of His way!

Sarah followed my directions and did everything that was asked of her. She was willing to fight for her husband. I want to be clear that this could have ended badly, and not all situations will turn out as hers did. In the end the thing that was keeping Hank from hitting rock bottom was Sarah staying with him and covering for him. Once his wife of over thirty years left, things changed. She was brave enough to expose her husband's hidden sin. She was tired of hiding things, had enough of pretending like everything was okay, and finally did something about it. I will be 100% honest with you—when she made that first step, things got tough and it was very scary for her. But she was finally free and out of the way.

I worked with Sarah and her family through this battle. I also visited Hank in the hospital during the worst part of his recovery. I can say that a spouse leaving is many times the thing that brings the addict to rock bottom. See, Hank had Sarah under his control, but even in addiction he loved her. When she left him all he could think about was getting her

4 • STOP COVERING FOR THEM

back. He was willing to go to treatment only after he realized she wasn't coming back. She blocked his phone calls and refused to let him control her. She would've never done that if it wasn't for her following instructions and exposing him. Sarah said something in her testimony that rings true: "Wisdom without obedience is just advice."

> **WISDOM WITHOUT OBEDIENCE IS JUST ADVICE**

Yes, it was scary. Yes, it was ugly. Hank hit an all-time low in his life, but in the end it turned out better than anyone could have expected. Hank and Sarah now serve together at Freeway Ministries, they are active in a local church, and Hank has years of clean time. Listen to what Sarah said about her relationship with Hank now.

> *Life is not all peaches and cream. It's hard because of the consequences of sin and bad choices. But I do have a new man now! One who is clean and sober, who will NOT steal a dime anymore, who won't lie to me, who doesn't get angry with me, and who wouldn't say an unkind word to me! WOW! He reads his Bible every morning unprompted and won't listen to any worldly music. I don't have anything to cover up anymore! But he does know I won't do that any longer.*

The enabler who covers for the addict can often be the person hindering change in the addict's life. If you're struggling with covering for a loved one, I encourage you to read Sarah's full testimony in the Appendix.

4 • STOP COVERING FOR THEM

WORKING THROUGH THIS CHAPTER

IDENTIFYING THE PROBLEM

Loving someone is not making them feel good, turning a blind eye, agreeing with their sin, or covering for them while they sin. The person who covers for the addict is involved in and responsible for the consequences of using. Remember that you are involved when you act like you don't know or cover for them in any way. You may not be lying, but if you're not being totally transparent about the situation, you're still covering. I cannot help but be reminded of James 4:17: "So whoever knows the right thing to do and fails to do it, for him it is sin" (ESV). Just stop covering for them. As my friend, Pastor Kevin Baker, said, "John, we are not responsible for what we don't know, but for what we do know." Friend, you and I are responsible for what we know. We're not talking about having a gossip-fest or trying to involve people just to involve them—they have to be part of the problem or part of the solution. We are practicing Matthew 18:15-17 and Galatians 6:1-5. You are the one called to reach out to that person caught in the snare of sin (Galatians 6:1-2). I challenge you to study these sections of God's Word and learn from them.

4 • STOP COVERING FOR THEM

BREAKING THE PATTERN

In her testimony, Sarah mentioned feeling like she was in prison when she was covering for Hank. Right now, someone reading this book feels trapped in the prison of someone else's addiction. Friend, you cannot control the actions of a grownup, but you sure can stop covering for them. How would you respond to the news of having terminal cancer? You would treat it seriously, and this is just as serious! How a person responds to an illness like cancer is the way you must respond to someone in active addiction. Are you wanting to actually do something about this or do you just want advice? Review the Scriptures, pray for discernment, talk to your pastor, then prayerfully confront the addict with a gentle spirit. Do the right thing before it is too late. Here are suggested steps to follow.

- Make sure you've built a relationship with the addict before you talk with them so they know you love them and want the best for them. I'm embarrassed to admit that I've made the mistake of not following that advice more than once and I regret it.
- Make sure you've done what you can to confront the addict in love, pleading with them to get help. Remember, Sarah waited thirteen years. My point is not to get you to wait that long, but to make sure you know the addict is refusing to get help on their own.

4 • STOP COVERING FOR THEM

- Make a commitment to not be a part of their addiction ever again. Make today the day you no longer allow this person to include you in the lies and deceit. Breaking this pattern of covering will be so freeing for you.
- Think of all the people who were there to pray for Sarah who previously had no clue what was going on and the support, comfort, and encouragement she received from them. Pray for discernment about who you should ask to help you when it comes time to expose your loved one — "the troops." Start a list of people you know who can help. Remind yourself you don't want to be guilty of covering for them if something was to happen and you knew but didn't tell those who could help. Honestly, it's unfair to you to have to carry that kind of responsibility around.
- Take the next step and reach out to the troops. Plan a meeting and talk to them all at once so you don't have to do it repeatedly. You also don't want the story to get mixed up and have people confuse what you said. Just doing it once will be painful enough.
- Prepare yourself for the worst. Know that when you do this you have to be ready for everything that comes with exposing them — the phone calls, the threats of suicide, the dangers of the addict, and possibly even them ending their life. It's tough but it's the truth.
- Learn about restraining orders and how to go about psychiatric holds in your area. I tell families to place them on a ninety-six hour hold in our area, then I'll visit them in the hospital after they sleep a while.

4 • STOP COVERING FOR THEM

Some may not agree with what I'm advising and that is your prerogative. But, I have seen this be effective many times—I know what works. Sarah mentioned the pain in her testimony and that pain is real. This is going to be one of the hardest things you have ever done. Remember, what happens once you expose them is not your fault regardless of the consequences.

MOVING FORWARD

Stand your ground and don't give in. When you knowingly hide your loved one's addiction, you're keeping the others who love this person in the dark. As a follower of Christ, you're called to walk in the light. What would've happened if Sarah continued to hide Hank's situation? According to Sarah, he would be dead. If you're a part of keeping someone's addiction a secret in any way, what happens when that person dies? Exposing the addict takes you out of the way. I am praying over this as I write and hope you don't have to experience that kind of guilt.

4 • STOP COVERING FOR THEM

REFLECTION QUESTIONS

Answer these questions in a notebook to help you think about and apply the concepts in this chapter.

1. What secrets are you keeping for the addict?
2. List the pride issues that may cause you to cover for the person you're trying to help.
3. How does the addict's life need to be "ruined" for the chains of addiction to be broken? How are you keeping that from happening?
4. What wisdom is God giving you that you're unwilling to obey?
5. Take time to examine your prayers. Are you praying more for the addict or are you asking God to show you what steps of obedience you must take?
6. What counsel are you receiving but unwilling to follow?
7. List the people available to support you. Or are you doing this alone?
8. What is your hope for the person you're trying to help?

5

STOP PARENTING OUT OF GUILT

Ezekiel 18:20 (ESV)
The soul who sins shall die. The son shall not suffer for the iniquity of the father, nor the father suffer for the iniquity of the son. The righteousness of the righteous shall be upon himself, and the wickedness of the wicked shall be upon himself.

Philippians 3:13 (ESV)
Brothers, I do not consider that I have made it my own. But one thing I do: forgetting what lies behind and straining forward to what lies ahead,

One of the things God has called me to do is evangelism, and with that calling comes traveling, sometimes taking me through my hometown. Just driving through Jefferson City makes my stomach turn, bringing back insecurities, guilt, and shame. See, that is the place I used to

5 • STOP PARENTING OUT OF GUILT

"run and gun." I was a bad person back then and have many memories I'm not proud of nor will I boast in. When I see someone I knew from my drug addict days, guilt and shame about my past often affect how I approach and talk to them. Instead of interacting with them like the forgiven child of God I know I am, guilt tugs at my emotions, bringing me down with the weight of my past. My emotional reaction in this situation is very similar to the emotional reaction that causes someone to parent out of guilt. I cannot tell you how many times I talk with parents who are classic enablers because they feel guilty about their past parenting. I counsel parents who treat their grown children differently than they would anyone else, not just because of a parental bond, but because of past guilt and shame.

Let me play the scene out for you. You're a parent or parental figure in someone's life. You have something from your past that keeps you in "fixer mode" in regard to this person. It may be something like a past lifestyle of addiction, abuse, abandonment, adultery—you name it—and you feel like it's your fault that your son or daughter is struggling with addiction. Maybe you and your spouse split up when your son or daughter was young and you feel like your divorce caused the pain resulting in their addiction. You're clean, sober, and living a decent life with morals, but when you see their pain you feel guilty about it. You're trying to pay them back for what you think you did to them by trying to fix their problems with your time, money, a place to live, and material things. You bail them out of jail, pay their phone bill, buy them a car, and let them live in your house even though it never works out and causes problems with their stepdad or stepmom. Why are you doing this? Because you feel ashamed and guilty for something you did in the past and you're trying to make up for it by enabling them.

There are two questions I like to ask families who are struggling with enablement: What can you do about this situation? What can you change? One of the things you cannot change is the past. Many times parents (especially the mom) will continue to make emotional decisions due to some kind of guilt about the past. This is a  horrible way of thinking that will leave you stuck in a destructive cycle. Notice what Tammy, an enabling mother, says in her testimony.

> *I was not a good mom when my son was young because I was struggling with my own addiction. I have spent the rest of his life trying to make up for it and in the process was assisting him in killing himself. My son has struggled with addiction off and on for many years and my guilt was so great that I thought if I gave him money and let him live with me for free it would somehow make up for the past. He has lived with me most of his adult life, rarely having a job, and if he did, never contributing to the bills. I gave him money whenever he asked, even though I knew what he was doing with it. I would give him my debit card to go to the*

5 • STOP PARENTING OUT OF GUILT

store and he would get himself cash without asking or telling me.

Does this sound like someone you know? Please pay attention! We all mess up and make mistakes, but I want to make sure you see that Tammy was trying to atone for her own sin by enabling her son. That's like trying to earn your salvation. It's never going to work.

> TRYING TO ATONE FOR YOUR OWN SIN WILL NEVER WORK

This hits close to home for me. My wife and I both have a past we're not proud of. Before becoming a Christian I was a bad person who did things I'm now ashamed of and I can say the same for Sharla. She struggles in the same way Tammy does. I thank God we never dealt with any of our kids while we were on drugs, but guilt has affected our parenting nonetheless. Sharla came to our marriage with two teenagers and I came with a four-year-old little boy. My son never saw me in addiction but had been through horrible situations before I got custody of him. I still feel guilty for what Keith had to go through and if I'm not careful, this will affect my decision making as a parent. Sharla also struggles with guilt from her past. My wife was fully occupied with her addiction and neglected to be the mother to her biological children that she is today. Sharla has repented from that life, no longer lives that way, and has asked Chase and Ashlyn to forgive her. While writing this chapter I had to stop and have a conversation with her about parenting out of guilt. She spoke

5 • STOP PARENTING OUT OF GUILT

of a letter she received while in rehab. Ashlyn wrote, "Mom, you taught me what not to do growing up." *Ouch.* Sharla still struggles with shame about this and it will continue to be a battle full of emotions that may never fully go away.

You cannot let the past define you as a parent any more than someone in recovery should allow their past to define them. I have nothing against recovery meetings that are not Christ-centered. I personally don't go to them, but know many who have done well through them and still go today. With that being said, I don't introduce myself as an addict. I will never shake your hand and say, "Hello, my name is John and I am an addict." I personally don't keep track of the days since the last time I used drugs either. I feel that's almost like a countdown to a person's next time using. Let me say again if you keep track of your days and introduce yourself as an addict as part of your recovery, that is your prerogative. But not calling myself an addict is part of my pressing forward and forgetting those things which are behind (Philippians 3:13).

I would encourage you to commit to memorizing some of God's promises to remind you—if you're a follower of Christ—your past is covered by the blood of Jesus and you're now walking in forgiveness. One of my favorite sections of Scripture is Colossians 1:21-22. I have committed it to memory to help me deal with past guilt and shame.

And you, who once were alienated and enemies in your mind by wicked works, yet now He has reconciled in the body of His flesh through death, to present you holy, and blameless, and above reproach in His sight—
(NKJV)

5 • STOP PARENTING OUT OF GUILT

Warren Wiersbe said it best: "Most Christians are crucified between two thieves. The guilt of yesterday and the worries of tomorrow." Friend, center your parenting on God's Word and allow the past to be left at the cross, not to be brought up again. As far as the east is from the west you have been forgiven. Your identity is not in your past but is found in the person and finished work of Jesus Christ. Did you read that? You are found in Christ and your identity is in Him, not in your past (see Romans 6). If you are allowing guilt, shame, and insecurities from your past to affect sound judgment, you have to focus on your walk with God, understand your righteous position in Christ, and make sure you're being obedient to do your part. Can you change what you've done? What can you do about it?

> YOUR IDENTITY IS FOUND IN JESUS CHRIST, NOT YOUR PAST

Not only will your own emotions tug on you, but children know how to pour on the guilt to manipulate you too. They will use the past against you time and time again. Read what Tammy had to say.

> *I started going to Freeway in December of 2016. John and Sharla counseled me for well over a year about how I was enabling my son, but I couldn't quit. My guilt was so huge I felt like I owed it to him. In February of 2018 I finally had enough. The verbal abuse was just too much. I moved and completely cut him off financially.*

5 • STOP PARENTING OUT OF GUILT

Tammy finally had enough and moved past her guilt. Regardless of what her son does now he will have to face the consequences for it. She will always struggle with guilt, but it won't control her anymore. Her decision making is not controlled by her emotions.

Notice the Scriptures used at the beginning of the chapter. Your children are not guilty for your sins. Stop letting the past define you, your children, and how you parent them. As a follower of Christ you have been forgiven for your sins. It is very important for you to seek forgiveness from those your addiction has affected. Whether it is your children, parents, grandchildren, or whoever, you cannot keep reliving that sin over and over again. If you're trying to make up for the bad example you set, the last thing you should do is enable your children. Remember what Tammy said in her testimony: "I have spent the rest of his life trying to make up for it and in the process was assisting him in killing himself." I want you to know that I am praying for everyone who reads this book; that God would free you from that guilt and give you the strength to stop parenting out of it. In doing so, you are literally loving your children to the grave. But can I encourage you? Today is a new day. If you are a Christian you are forgiven, and your past is buried in the tomb with Christ.

You may be saying, "If I don't help them, they will be homeless or maybe they will die." Both statements are correct, but here is the honest truth: they are more likely to die from your enabling than if you stop enabling them now. You cannot change the past or make up for what you've done.

5 • STOP PARENTING OUT OF GUILT

What you *can* do is the right thing now. Take charge and refuse to parent out of guilt. Shame should not be the motivation behind your parenting. Your motivation should be what is right. This will be one of the hardest things you will ever have to do, but there will be no change in the situation unless you stop enabling. Know that it will get worse before it gets better. Prepare yourself for the guilt trips, the phone calls, the other family members who don't understand, the threats of suicide, and the, "If you were really a Christian, you wouldn't do this to me!" taunts. This is what Tammy said concerning the difficulty of cutting off her son.

> **DO THE RIGHT THING NOW: REFUSE TO PARENT OUT OF GUILT**

> *It was the hardest thing I have ever done. He was soon evicted and was homeless, couch surfing, or sleeping in his car. John and Sharla helped me stay strong and I refused to let him stay with me or give him any money. It was heartbreaking. I had to let God have him.*

It was the hardest thing she'd ever done. It took well over a year for Tammy to do the right thing and it is still hard for her. This was the first time I had ever seen a parent move out of their own house and stop paying the bills in order to stop enabling their child.

At first, he laid on the guilt and threw her faith in her face. But this is what it took for him to hit his rock bottom. She wanted to rescue him a thousand times, but she stood her ground. She is now enjoying her life as a single woman. She

5 • STOP PARENTING OUT OF GUILT

no longer has to walk on eggshells dealing with the issues that come from a son in addiction living under her roof. There is not a surprise waiting for her every day when she gets home and she is happier than she's been in a long time. Here's what happened next.

> *He now has his own apartment and I can't remember the last time he asked for money. Our relationship is so much better now and he is supporting himself. I have peace in my heart regarding the past and I know that I will never assist him in killing himself which is what I was doing. He is a kind and loving son again and no longer acts like I owe him. I am forever grateful for the council and support I received from my Freeway family. I feel like a huge burden has been lifted off of me.*

I wish I could say that he is plugged in with us at church, but he hasn't quite gotten there yet. We are believing God to move in that situation as well. Yes, there are struggles and always will be. The truth of the matter is that we are in a long-distance run, not a short sprint. We are all walking through life together and we all stumble from time to time, but we help each other up.

5 • STOP PARENTING OUT OF GUILT

WORKING THROUGH THIS CHAPTER

IDENTIFYING THE PROBLEM

Guilt about your past causes you to make emotional parenting decisions that could enable your child's addiction. Stop parenting out of guilt.

BREAKING THE PATTERN

If you're struggling with guilt from the past, please give that to God in prayer right now. Stop reading this book and get alone with God to pray. He is a loving and forgiving God. Remember, we all have sinned and fallen short of the glory of God. If you have never apologized to your son or daughter, you should do that. Once you have apologized, don't keep bringing it up. It's not about how you start but how you finish. This is a lifelong battle and you need to prepare yourself for it. Remember, people in active addiction are the best manipulators. They will do and say whatever they can to hurt you. What happens if you allow them to draw you into the blame game? You will end up creating someone with an entitlement mentality. The more you feed into the blame game the more you keep them feeling entitled. Blaming yourself will only make you feel more guilty and feeling more guilty will keep you parenting out of guilt.

A parent whose decisions are controlled by guilt is just like a driver who's too impaired to drive—your judgment is skewed to the point of making bad decisions. Instead of parenting out of guilt, please follow these suggestions.

- Look at your situation from a biblical perspective. Find Scripture that will help you overcome the guilt from your past then commit it to memory. Here are some good verses to start with: 1 John 1:9; Philippians 3:13-14; Galatians 2:20-21; 2 Corinthians 5:17-19; and Luke 9:62. Preach these Scriptures to yourself when you want to give in.

- Make parental decisions from a biblical point of view. Let God's Word dictate your decisions in helping your loved one, not guilt. Before you start to help your loved one, get counsel from godly friends who understand addiction and are not emotionally involved in the situation.

- Develop concrete policies outlining what you will and won't do for your loved one and don't allow yourself to break them. If you say you're not going to do something, like letting them stay with you, for example, then don't do it.

- Read Chapter 7, "Start Investing." Use the principles in that chapter to help your children without enabling them.

- Email us at Freeway Ministries and let us help you. Please see our contact information at the end of the book.

5 • STOP PARENTING OUT OF GUILT

▶ MOVING FORWARD

The trouble with those of us who have a rough past is the things people say about us are often true. I will be out in public and have someone look at me like, *I know* you, then they come my way. The conversation goes something like this: "Do you remember me?" I say, "No, but was it B.C., or A.C.?" Then they look at me with a strange expression. I proceed with, "B.C. is before Christ, and A.C. is after Christ." See, I'm not the same person I was before I met Christ. So, regardless of the messes I made then I cannot allow those things to affect my decision making now. I cannot change what I've done and neither can you, so let's quit trying.

So what's holding you back? Like Tammy, sometimes parents need to be reminded that they're helping their children kill themselves. Stop allowing the past to affect your parenting in the present. As a Christian, God doesn't bring up your past again, so why should you? Notice Tammy said she was trying to make up for what she'd done in the past. The hard truth is you cannot pay for your sins. You will never be able to make up for the past in that way. You can buy a thousand cars, pay all their bills, and still not change what's been done. Stop trying to atone for your sins. Own it and move forward. Today is a new day, and as long as there is breath in your lungs you can stop parenting out of guilt.

5 • STOP PARENTING OUT OF GUILT

REFLECTION QUESTIONS

Answer these questions in a notebook to help you think about and apply the concepts in this chapter.

1. What parenting mistakes do you still feel guilty about? Does this guilt result in enablement? If so, how?
2. How do you think your enabling actions make up for your past mistakes as a parent?
3. Make a list of ten of God's promises in Scripture and memorize them.
4. What worries about tomorrow cause you to enable the child or person you are trying to help, hoping they will not make another mistake?
5. Why do you think you can change what you've done in the past?
6. What do you need to say and physically act on to show you are not enabling your child?
7. Have you sought forgiveness from your child for past parenting mistakes? If so, have you moved on and left those mistakes in the past?
8. Do you need to seek forgiveness from the only One who can forgive and then move on?

6
ROCK BOTTOM IS A GREAT PLACE TO START OVER

2 Corinthians 7:10 (ESV)
For godly grief produces a repentance that leads to salvation without regret, whereas worldly grief produces death.

Isaiah 55:7 (ESV)
Let the wicked forsake his way, and the unrighteous man his thoughts; let him return to the Lord, that he may have compassion on him, and to our God, for he will abundantly pardon.

I recently spoke to a mother who is very involved in a support group for families who have loved ones in active addiction. She and her daughter have been estranged for three years and she is currently raising her grandchildren. Her daughter is in the psychiatric ward of a local hospital once again. Though I could hear the desperation in this

6 • ROCK BOTTOM IS A GREAT PLACE TO START OVER

woman's voice, she also had lots of wisdom from experience in dealing with her daughter. She said she couldn't let her come home because she is a danger to her own children. She couldn't give her any money because she knew it might be used to purchase drugs. This lady was speaking my language! She understood addiction and was doing what I would tell her to do. I was like, "Go, momma!" I told her that I was very proud of her and that she was doing the right thing. Then she said something that struck me. "I physically hurt because I don't know what may happen to my daughter. My bones ache at night because I know she is prostituting and being raped, but I cannot help her."

That is the heartbreaking part. As the family of the addict, you're in pain because of their addiction and can't help. This chapter is one of the toughest for a parent to read because you want to rescue your child. You care about them, so you want to do what family does—feed them, clothe them, protect them, give them shelter, and help them out in any way you can. But, doing those things can hinder your loved one from getting to the place where they can defeat their addiction: rock bottom.

What is rock bottom and what is its purpose? <u>Rock bottom is a place of surrender and submission.</u> The thing many people don't understand is that it doesn't always take the worst situation a person has been in to hit their rock bottom. It is also important to know that someone can hit rock bottom even if they have been through tougher times in the

6 • ROCK BOTTOM IS A GREAT PLACE TO START OVER

past. Rock bottom is whatever situation that brings someone to a place of surrender. I'd be a wealthy man if I had a dollar for every time I heard someone say, "They have to be at rock bottom now because it doesn't get any lower than this. They've lost everything." The sad truth is your loved one may not even *have* a rock bottom.

> **ROCK BOTTOM IS A PLACE OF SURRENDER AND SUBMISSION**

A biblical example of rock bottom is given to us by God in the flesh Himself. In Luke 15, Jesus tells parables about three lost things to defend himself for eating with the tax collectors and other sinners: a lost sheep, a lost coin, and a lost son. The son is only known as the prodigal son. In our language we would call him the wasteful son. Now someone reading this book is saying, "I know one of those!" This was the younger of two sons who represented the tax collectors and sinners who were the worst of the worst in Jesus' day. The prodigal son was a spoiled brat in my opinion—someone who thought he deserved something for nothing. He thought he was entitled to his "fair share" which wasn't really his at all. I want you to stop right now and read Luke 15:11-32 a couple of times. Picture your loved one as the wasteful son. Notice what happens when the prodigal leaves with the money and meets up with his friends from the far country—he wastes it all and then there's a famine in the land. You say, "I have lived through that more than once with my child." Once the money is gone, the friends are gone. The son finds

6 • ROCK BOTTOM IS A GREAT PLACE TO START OVER

himself alone, hungry, and in the worst possible place a Hebrew boy could be: the pigpen. Sound familiar?

What does the father in the story do? Does he chase his son down? Does he go after him into the far country and put up prodigal missing posters? No, he waits on the porch for his son to come to a place of surrender. The prodigal had to be in the pigpen before that would happen. That stinky, filthy, lonely, shameful, and humiliating place was where he needed to be. His dad didn't come and bail him out, but waited for him on the porch.

> **THE FATHER DIDN'T BAIL OUT THE PRODIGAL; HE WAITED FOR HIM ON THE PORCH**

Just what happened in that pigpen? The son had time to think things over. We call it "a come to Jesus" moment or rock bottom. My moment came in a prison cell on a hot summer day in Fulton, Missouri at 32 years of age. I needed that prison cell, Jacob needed that wrestling match, the prodigal needed that pigpen, and your loved one needs to be where God can get them alone to surrender in submission. What if the prodigal's father would have jumped the gun and stopped this from happening? What if he would've gone out looking to rescue him? The son needed to be there in that pigpen because it was in that lonely, lowly place that he "came to himself." He woke up from his false reality and realized how good he had it (Luke 15:17). Reflecting on the kindness of his father he said three "I wills": I will arise, I will go, I will say (Luke 15:18). He climbed out of the pigpen all by himself and journeyed home.

I can see the son nervously rehearsing his apology on the way. He knows he's the talk of the village and is humiliated by his sin. I can also see his dad waiting in the same place on the porch every day, watching the road to the far country hoping his son would come home. When he finally sees his son returning, he runs to meet him where he is, which is at his place of repentance. The son starts his apology and gets to the part where he is going to ask his father to make him a slave when suddenly he is interrupted by his father. The son is then dressed in the best clothing with sandals placed on his dirty, bare feet and the father calls for a celebration because he has returned. See, friend, you have to wait on the porch like the father. You have to let your loved one come to a place of brokenness—their rock bottom—before you can help them.

Let me give you a real-life example. I met a man named Barry in 2011. Barry had been stabbed, pinned between a building and a car, in prison many times, and even lost his mother, but none of those things was rock bottom for Barry. When I met him he was living with a woman he sold drugs to. She was a lady who had a good job, a house, and came from a good family. The police kicked her door in one night to arrest Barry. They took her kid from her and she lost her career. She bonded Barry out and not long after that he was released. Upon his release he started using drugs again. She told him she was going to leave him behind if he kept

6 • ROCK BOTTOM IS A GREAT PLACE TO START OVER

using. This was finally Barry's rock bottom. Barry ended up giving his life to Jesus and marrying that lady. They have been married and clean since 2011. Now Barry and his wife are doing great. They're very involved in recovery ministry at Freeway and are raising their kids in church.

So what happened to Barry that brought him to rock bottom? It's not necessarily the severity of a situation that does it, but just the point in a person's life when they've had enough. Barry and God had to wrestle to get to the place of surrender. No one would have thought Barry's rock bottom would be something like this after all he'd already been through. That's why I say you never know when a person will have had enough. All you can do is stop enabling them and stop hindering rock bottom from happening.

> YOU NEVER KNOW WHEN A PERSON WILL HAVE HAD ENOUGH

I promise that your loved one will never hit rock bottom living off you or your family—they won't change because they don't have to. Some say, "I told them they're going to have to leave. I've had enough of them freeloading off of me." Many times enablers remind me of that dysfunctional family in the toy section of Walmart. Do you know that family? You see this kid throwing a temper tantrum in the middle of the aisle. They're screaming, yelling, crying, spitting, and whatever else they can think of because the parent isn't giving them what they want. The parent warns the kid over and over again and then they start the countdown. It goes something like this: "Jimmy, if you don't stop you're going to be in big trouble. I'm going to spank your backside if you keep it up." Then after the child doesn't comply, they start counting. "One... two... three... four...." Enablers are like that parent counting down in Walmart. The child is a perfect picture of a grownup who has no respect for the parent or other authority figure. They've heard all the threats before and know they don't have to pay it any attention because the person who makes the threat doesn't ever follow through.

I remember preaching outside in Salem, Missouri one July. It was high noon and the heat was on! There wasn't any shade for me to preach under and I got a nice sunburn. I felt really sorry for the worship team. While there, I met a small group of people who do recovery ministry in that area. They are a really neat bunch and on fire for the Lord. Many of them have a story to tell, but there was one lady I can't forget because of her attractive joy. She was glowing with her excitement and devotion for Jesus and she loved to help people make it through addiction. By looking at her you could tell this lady had lived a rough life. She told me she had been in a local treatment center over twenty times before she finally had enough. Did you get that? Over twenty times, friend! What happened to this lady? Was the last time in the treatment center the worst? Maybe, but what about all the other times?

Listen, we can never tell what it will take for someone to come to their rock bottom, but we have a choice—we can either hinder it from happening or help bring it about. Rock bottom is when a person has nothing earthly left to depend on and that is where they have a better chance to hear from God. I have parents call me who want to bond their children out of the jail cell. That is the worst thing you can do because jail is a wonderful place to hit rock bottom. Remember, rock bottom isn't a place, but a state of mind. Jail can be the place where a person comes to their rock bottom. You cannot quit jail, but you can quit rehab. You've never heard of someone getting shot because they were breaking into someone's house while in jail. People don't go on high-speed chases while in jail. Jail isn't rock bottom but God has used many jail cells to bring people to a place of brokenness and repentance. There are plenty of bad things that can happen to an addict—jail, prison, rehab, bankruptcy, divorce, losing children, deaths, and many other things—but those bad things may not be rock bottom. It's simply whatever makes you say, "That is enough. I am done."

> ROCK BOTTOM ISN'T A PLACE, BUT A STATE OF MIND

Rock bottom's purpose isn't to punish the addict because addiction and sin are punishment enough. The Bible is clear that the "wages of sin is death, but the free gift of God is eternal life in Christ Jesus our Lord" (Romans 6:23, ESV). Instead, the purpose of rock bottom is repentance as a result of humility. Repentance is a total change in behavior. Godly sorrow brings repentance. The purpose of rock bottom is to bring about a godly sorrow that brings repentance and true change in one's life.

6 • ROCK BOTTOM IS A GREAT PLACE TO START OVER

Paul wrote to the church at Corinth about a discipline issue. They had to ask someone to leave fellowship and it was tough. Paul wrote to them concerning the purpose of the discipline and said it was the thing God used to change that person's life (see 2 Corinthians 7:8-10). Rock bottom is a place of surrender that oftentimes defeats pride. It is hard to be proud when you are sleeping under a bridge, hungry without a way to eat, dirty, stinky, hopeless, and alone. The addict must come to themselves just like the prodigal son and wake up from the world of enablement. That will only happen through a rock bottom experience. The person consumed by addiction needs to be humbled, broken, and stripped of everything keeping them high and numb. God operates through humility, and humility comes through being at a place of surrender. Please read the Scriptures below and see how they speak into this situation, linking brokenness and humility with blessing.

James 4:6 (ESV)
But he gives more grace. Therefore it says,
"God opposes the proud but gives grace to the humble."

James 4:10 (ESV)
Humble yourselves before the Lord, and he will exalt you.

Psalm 51:17 (ESV)
The sacrifices of God are a broken spirit;
a broken and contrite heart, O God, you will not despise.

6 • ROCK BOTTOM IS A GREAT PLACE TO START OVER

WORKING THROUGH THIS CHAPTER

IDENTIFYING THE PROBLEM

The addict usually isn't ready to change until they reach their rock bottom. Hindering someone from reaching rock bottom by enabling them could lead to their final ruin.

There are three kinds of excuses a person makes when they haven't yet hit rock bottom: relational, material, and geographical. Ask your loved one, "Are you willing to do whatever it takes?" If they say, "Yes, *but*..." they are not ready. The excuses go away when you hit rock bottom. Bad relationships are let go of when they come to that place of surrender. Material things don't matter when they've had enough. When a person is really ready to submit themselves to change, they will go anywhere you tell them.

Are you cushioning someone's fall, keeping them from rock bottom? You may be killing them if that is the case, friend. I'm telling you this because I care about you. It's not your responsibility to repent, convince, or convict them of sin. It is your responsibility to not be the enabler in their life. Remember, rock bottom is different for everyone, and we never know what it will take for the person to finally humble themselves and repent. Rock bottom may be losing your license or going to jail for the first time. It could be a near-death experience, embarrassment, or losing contact with

6 • ROCK BOTTOM IS A GREAT PLACE TO START OVER

family. Sometimes people don't have a rock bottom because they refuse to stop using. Rock bottom may be a funeral, and that is the sad truth of addiction. I have had about every situation you can imagine happen, and sometimes rock bottom is a grave. Do your part to keep from enabling them and pray they come to a place of brokenness. Never give up. As long as they have breath there is a chance that one day they may come to a place of surrender and you can be there to help when they do.

BREAKING THE PATTERN

Are you helping or hindering rock bottom from happening in someone's life? Think back to the times you thought you were helping and ended up hindering them. Remember, if you keep doing what you've always done, you'll keep getting what you've always gotten. Here are some suggestions to help rock bottom happen.

- Let them sit in jail. Refuse to bond them out, do not put money on their books, and don't hire them a lawyer. They did the crime and they can deal with the consequences. They are not going to starve to death. Listen, I was in county jail off and on for at least two years of my life with no money. I did a year and a half in prison with $5 a month on my books and not one visit, let alone a phone call. Guess what? I survived, but it broke me. I would not be where I am today without it.

6 • ROCK BOTTOM IS A GREAT PLACE TO START OVER

- Stop taking the phone calls. If they're in active addiction but not willing to respond to your instructions (see the next chapter for more details), you really don't have anything to talk about. They're demonstrating they're not willing to change. Remember, you're calling the shots if they want your help. Have you raised your child? Then don't let them keep you up all night answering the phone. Quit treating that grown man or woman like a child. Let them figure it out. Turn off the phone or block their number.
- Stop giving them rides. Remember Grandpa Tom? He had to learn this the hard way. Grandpa Tom had to come out of retirement and get a job due to all the money his grandson cost him. Today Tom doesn't allow his grandson to call the shots. The grandson hasn't hit rock bottom yet, but we are still hopeful. Running someone in active addiction all over town like a taxicab isn't helping them, I promise. You may not be able to keep them from running the streets, but you can refuse to give them a ride. You're driving them from dope house to dope house, and most likely helping them transport drugs from one place to the next. I remember doing all kinds of horrible things, running from one crime scene to the next with someone else's parents unwittingly giving us a ride.
- I know someone reading this is thinking, *I can't sleep wondering if they're out in the cold without a place to go.* My advice to you is don't sleep then! You have to take a stand some day or they will most likely never hit rock bottom while you're alive to enable them.

6 • ROCK BOTTOM IS A GREAT PLACE TO START OVER

Whenever you're tempted to enable them, ask yourself these questions:
- What is the purpose of rock bottom?
- Why is rock bottom important?
- If I do this will I hinder them or help them in their recovery?
- Are they calling the shots, or am I?

Pray about it and seek wise counsel from someone who can help who is not emotionally involved. You can do this!

 **MOVING FORWARD**

Stop buying into excuses from now on. Set up boundaries for yourself and figure out exactly what your help will look like from now on. Remember, do not let the person in active addiction call the shots and dictate how you are going to help them. Prepare yourself, have people praying for you, and seek counsel from someone who can guide you through this. You need people who are not emotionally or relationally involved in this situation to help you make wise decisions. Your loved one cannot hit rock bottom unless you stop enabling them. Tell yourself, *This is not to punish them, but to bring them to a place of humility. Humility is used by God to bring about change.* Don't give up on the person because rehab or jail didn't work, yet again. Rock bottom is a state of mind, not a place, so don't give up.

6 • ROCK BOTTOM IS A GREAT PLACE TO START OVER

REFLECTION QUESTIONS

Answer these questions in a notebook to help you think about and apply the concepts in this chapter.

1. Read 2 Corinthians 7:10-11. Define the characteristics of godly sorrow.
2. What wisdom do you have in helping an addict?
3. Have you hit your own rock bottom in trying to help the person you love?
4. How do you continue to impede the one you love from coming to a place of surrender?
5. What will it take for you to wait on the porch like the father did for the prodigal son?
6. How are you like the parent with a child throwing a tantrum in Walmart?
7. Have you asked your loved one, "Are you willing to do whatever it takes?" What was their response? Was there a "but"?
8. Identify and examine the excuses the person you're helping is making and how they fit into the material, relational, and geographical categories.

7
START INVESTING

John 10:27 (ESV)
My sheep hear my voice,
and I know them, and they follow me.

Matthew 10:38 (ESV)
And whoever does not take his cross
and follow me is not worthy of me.

I'm not a rich man, but I do understand a little bit about investments. A smart person invests their money in an asset that has the best return. Imagine that you save a little money and then meet with a professional about investing it. You look at the average return on some stocks and find the three that have the highest ten-year average. I'm told the wise thing to do is divide your money between these three stocks.

7 • START INVESTING

That way you have a better chance of getting the best return—you know, the whole "not putting all your eggs in one basket" thing. Now imagine meeting with a broker and you're shown a stock that has a twenty-five percent average return for a ten-year period. That's the kind of investment you need to make! Then he shows you stocks that have never had a return, but instead are guaranteed to *lose* money if you invest in them. Would you invest? What if there was a stock with the potential to return a lot of money, but it also carried a risk of losing a lot of money? Those stocks might be worth a shot depending on the person investing, but it's never a good idea for anyone to buy into a stock that has a history of losing a person's investment.

You may be thinking, *Why is he talking about investments and stocks? What does this have to do with enabling addicts?* I'm speaking about making wise investments because that's how we need to approach helping a person in active addiction. Instead, you may be investing the wrong things and getting no return on your investment from your loved one. You've been paying out money, time, houses, cars, childcare, court costs, lawyers, gas, and so on, but seeing no change in your loved one—the return you're hoping for. I know this may sound harsh, but you might as well flush your money down the toilet or use it to start a campfire rather than giving it to an active drug addict. I want to help you learn how to make a real investment in your loved one's life that

7 • START INVESTING

will yield a good return, rather than just throwing your money away.

Look back to the Scripture at the beginning of this chapter in which Jesus said to follow Him. Imagine for a moment that Jesus is standing on the bank of the Sea of Galilee. He just finished saying something really powerful (because that's what Jesus did), then He asks the disciples to get in the boat to go to the other side. What if one of the disciples said, "I don't feel like going with you." Do you think Jesus would stop the boat, hold up the trip, and start trying to convince the disciple to get with the program? No! Jesus would leave that disciple on the bank and set sail without him. Don't get me wrong, I'm not saying to leave your loved one behind, but your motivation cannot be someone else's motivation. You're thinking, *What do I do, then?*

YOUR MOTIVATION CANNOT BE SOMEONE ELSE'S MOTIVATION

I want to share something I've learned through dealing with hundreds of families that's proven to work: invest instructions. When you invest instructions, the return on those instructions isn't money, but obedience. For example, just last night at Freeway Ministries a man from one of our local churches, Tony, brought his brother to the meeting. Tony's brother is in active addiction and had been playing games to manipulate his family. They have an ace in the hole though, and that ace is me. I've met with Tony and his parents, coaching them on what to do, and now they're using those tools to invest in this man's life. As a result, Tony

7 • START INVESTING

didn't give his brother money or allow him to dictate what was going to happen, but instead took control of the situation, investing the instruction to go with him to Freeway. He gave his brother a ride to our meeting where there was a hot meal, fellowship, and preaching from the Word of God. After the meeting, Tony offered to take his brother to a local homeless shelter. Tony called me later that night and I told him to get his brother a padlock (so his stuff wouldn't be stolen), then take him to the shelter.

Now look at what just happened there. Tony made an investment that had a return. The first investment was the offer to pick his brother up and bring him to a Freeway meeting. It's easy to hand someone a Freeway card and tell them they need to go to a meeting. There's nothing wrong with that, but Tony did more. He said, "I'll come and get you so we can go together." Tony didn't allow the active drug user to dictate the situation. His brother didn't want to come at first but decided to at the last minute. That is the return on the investment. The loved one in addiction responded to the investment with his obedience to the instructions and came to Freeway. He got in the car and came to the meeting! Then, Tony makes another investment by offering his brother a safe place to go other than the dope-house—a place that has structure and authority that won't enable him since the people at the shelter have zero emotional or relational attachment. Tony's brother responded to that investment with his willingness to go. Two for two is not a bad investment!

7 • START INVESTING

It's not that Tony doesn't care about his brother—just the opposite. He spent his money on gas and his time in coming to the meeting with his brother instead of spending that time with his wife and children. Now Tony's taking his brother to the shelter to check him in where he'll have the opportunity to prove he's serious about recovery. I want you to let this sink into your heart and mind. This is where many people fail to grab onto truth. Tony is giving his brother a chance to prove he's serious by making him follow instructions and do the work himself. We call this **obedience-based discipleship** and that is the only discipleship I find in the Bible.

> OBEDIENCE-BASED DISCIPLESHIP IS THE ONLY BIBLICAL KIND OF DISCIPLESHIP

Are you wondering what happened with these brothers? I texted back and forth with Tony until around midnight. At first his brother refused to follow the instructions, but at the last minute he agreed to go to the shelter. Tony checked him in and wanted to make sure there was a ride to pick his brother up for church in the morning. I told Tony to give his brother the number to Freeway transportation and make him do the calling—another investment of instructions. Tony's brother entered the shelter but ended up leaving. He had his "friends" come get him. Even though some may see this all as a waste, I see it as a win because there was some headway made and Tony learned a lesson about investing. Tony's brother eventually went back to the shelter and worked his way into the Freeway Ministries discipleship program. He's been on the road to recovery ever since. We've fought some battles with this man, but it's not over yet. He's sober, in church, has a job, and is part of his family again. Even if he doesn't make it through the program, there are a lot of positives that came from that one initial investment. At the meeting, he heard the Word of God preached and saw people with whom he could identify who were now clean and sober. Tony got a chance to talk with him about Jesus too, and we never know what those planted seeds will produce in the life of this man. Remember, it is not over for someone until they take their last breath. I am talking to the Christians reading this book. Don't limit God for the person in addiction. You are not responsible for the growing of the seed, just the planting.

I want to give you something else to think about. How hard does a drug addict have to work at their addiction? Dealers aren't just giving their drugs away, in case you didn't know. Drugs cost a lot of money and addicts have to work really hard to stay high. When they run out of money, their addiction doesn't just go away. That's when addicts turn into criminals and learn to hustle. Drug addicts will lose sleep, break their feet, go for days without eating, and push themselves to the limit to stay high. An addict will do whatever it takes to support their addiction, so if they refuse to work at their recovery, they aren't serious about it and won't put forth the effort once they enter a program.

> **HOW HARD DOES AN ADDICT HAVE TO WORK AT THEIR ADDICTION?**

7 • START INVESTING

Let me give you a scenario to think about for a moment. Freeway Ministries has discipleship housing for men and women who truly want to learn how to become a disciple of Jesus Christ. We invest instructions and they do the work. My job is to create an environment of change and they just have to take advantage of the opportunity by doing the work. When they follow the structure and truly surrender, their lives change dramatically. I can tell you story after story of people in whom God has done a radical work through our program. <u>Our program weeds out people who aren't serious about their recovery because we have a structure that's tough to follow for a person who isn't willing to do the work.</u> For instance, one rule is that our people have to put in five job applications a day until they get a job.

That rule came from my stay in the Salvation Army shelter in downtown Springfield, Missouri in 2009. My goal was to put in five applications a day until I got a job. I'd never turned on a computer and had no clue how to apply for anything online, so I thought I'd just apply in person. I would leave that shelter every morning and look for work. I had to be back by noon to feed the homeless, so my day started early. I will never forget my first day in the city on the busses. I remember it like it was yesterday. I walked down to the bus station from the shelter at 636 North Boonville Avenue. I sat on the concrete bench to wait for the bus and talked with the drivers when they came by. They told me all the busses end up at that same location no matter which one I got on. That was all I needed to know. My journey in Springfield began.

7 • START INVESTING

Talking to potential employers, I would say, "Give me the job no one wants and I will do it better than anyone has ever done it." I was rejected by so many people because of my appearance and availability—I could only work Monday through Friday due to the rules at the shelter. My only transportation was the city bus, but that didn't stop me. I remember people sitting in front of the TV at the shelter telling me, "You're wasting your time. There's no work out there. We've looked." That just made me look twice as hard! I was driven and hungry. I soon landed a job ringing a bell for the Salvation Army, and then while ringing that bell I got another job at a restaurant. That was over ten years ago and I haven't gone one day since then without being employed.

When someone is ready to change, their obedience to your instructions will be the return on your investment and the proof that they're ready to work at their recovery. When someone comes to me and says, "John, I want to enter your discipleship housing. I'm ready for help." If they're on the street, I put them in a shelter first and give them homework to prove they're willing to work at their recovery. Currently, I'm working with a guy living in a shelter. To prove him as serious, I gave him one week's worth of homework. I have him doing something every evening until we meet again this Saturday to see if he'll follow through. I never know who will end up following through and who will end up flaking out.

> **OBEDIENCE TO INSTRUCTIONS IS PROOF THAT SOMEONE'S READY TO WORK AT RECOVERY**

7 • START INVESTING

People can *tell* me they're serious and want to change—and I've heard about every story you can imagine—but it takes someone *showing* me they want to change by following my instructions and doing the work. Be an investor, but don't do the work for them. I've read my Bible every day since I was saved and I've never seen God use a lazy person to do anything. Make them do the work!

When I was sixteen my mom had a boyfriend named Don. Don was a kind person who basically did whatever my mom wanted him to. He purchased my first car for me but I didn't appreciate it at all. It was a Chevy Citation and I tore that thing up fast and in a hurry. I drove that car like it was stolen. I didn't appreciate it because I didn't have to work for it. It was given to me without me lifting a finger to pay for it.

When I became a husband, I also became a father to a young boy named Chase. He was thirteen when Sharla and I got married. It's been a rough road being a stepdad and Chase has been a tool in God's hand to humble me. I had no clue how to be a father to a teenage boy—let alone manage a blended family—but we have been together for over seven years now. When it came time for him to get a car, I remembered my experience with Don, so I told Chase he would have to work for it. I promised I would go half on his first car with him, so he started working at a local sandwich shop at fifteen. I found him a decent little used car and bought it. I didn't let him drive it until he paid for his half. He was and still is a hard worker and saved up the money. I made good on my part of the promise and Chase became the owner of a little Mazda. He learned a lesson that I never got to learn. Now he's a nineteen-year-old college student with a job at FedEx and is buying a newer car with his own money. He wouldn't be where he is today if we did it all for him.

And you cannot do the work for the addict either, so invest what will really help—the investment of instructions. Someone once said, "Don't wish for it, work for it." Through my experience of living life on the streets as one of the worst drug addicts you have ever met and being on the front lines in ministry, I believe this quote is true in recovery. You have to work hard and put skin in the game if you're going to overcome addiction. If someone will not work *toward* their recovery, they will not work once they are *in* recovery. Meditate on these Scriptures and remember that your loved one must not be lazy in their recovery. Make sure you're investing wisely and make them do the work!

2 Thessalonians 3:10 (ESV)
For even when we were with you, we would give you this command:
If anyone is not willing to work, let him not eat.

Proverbs 13:4 (ESV)
The soul of the sluggard craves and gets nothing,
while the soul of the diligent is richly supplied.

Proverbs 21:25 (ESV)
The desire of the sluggard kills him,
for his hands refuse to labor.

7 • START INVESTING

WORKING THROUGH THIS CHAPTER

IDENTIFYING THE PROBLEM

Friend, you have an investment issue. You're investing the wrong things in your loved one and not getting a return on those investments. Invest instructions and wait for their obedience as a return.

BREAKING THE PATTERN

Reread the story in this chapter about Tony who put his brother in a shelter. The investments he made really paid off. It can be easier to throw money at someone than it is to make the type of investment Tony made. The problem isn't investing itself, but *what* you're investing. Don't let the addict dictate what your help looks like. People who have been enabled are great manipulators and know how to work the heartstrings. Stop allowing them to guilt you into making emotional decisions that end up enabling them.

Think about the person you're trying to help. Are you investing in them or enabling them? Whatever you invest, make sure it requires effort and obedience on their part as a return. Make them do the work from now on. If you're struggling with knowing how to truly help, here are several ideas for simple investments that can have a huge return.

7 • START INVESTING

- The first tangible thing a person can invest is time. Love, according to Charles Stanley, is spelled T-I-M-E. Spend time with them.
- One of the things we've done as a family is have Christmas and Thanksgiving at our home for people who have nowhere to go. This is a wonderful experience. If the person is actively using, you may not want to bring them into your home, but I have been doing this since I had my first house in Springfield as a single father and I've never had any problems.
- I keep a book of bus passes in my car and if someone says they need a ride to work or cannot get somewhere to a recovery meeting I give them two bus passes. I also give them 50 cents for a transfer so they can use one bus pass on the way there and one on the way back.
- There are lots of clothing banks in town and I have no complex about wearing second-hand clothes, but there are a couple used items no one wants to wear: underwear and socks. You have no idea how degrading it is to wear used underwear. Take them to Walmart and spend $20 to get them new underwear and socks.
- Take them for a meal. One of the most rewarding things a person can do is take someone to a restaurant who hasn't been out to eat in years. I encourage those in ministry to pick up someone who has been in prison or jail for an extended time and take them out for a big, greasy cheeseburger. Get them supersized fries and a milkshake too. They will never forget you! It's rewarding to watch their pure enjoyment.

- Get them a cup of coffee.
- If they're not a member of your family, make them one! Addiction destroys families—people burn many bridges never to cross them again. I have just two pictures of my mother and one of my father. I never knew my dad and have felt alone for a very long time. I won't be able to regain all the things I lost because of my addiction, but when I got saved, God gave me a family in more ways than one. Having a family is something many never think they will ever have again and you can help fill that void.
- Birthdays are another big one. A birthday cake, ice cream, and maybe some gift cards for small amounts are great gifts. Many haven't ever had a healthy birthday party—birthdays and holidays are sometimes triggers that make a person want to use. Show them you can be sober and still have fun.
- Special occasions are another thing you can do for someone. I know a church that had a baby shower for a stripper. This changed her life, showing her the love that led her to quit stripping.
- Invest in good Bible study books to encourage them to learn. Take them to a Christian bookstore and buy them a journal, a study Bible, and a commentary, then teach them how to use them to grow.
- Take them camping, hunting, fishing, or teach them a trade.

7 • START INVESTING

▶ MOVING FORWARD

The hard truth is that your loved one might not be ready for recovery and may never change, but you have no way of knowing. Remember, you're not Jesus and can't change anyone. Read Chapter 2 again if you're struggling with this fact. Don't give up! Remember, you're not responsible for the return on the investment. You're a seed planter but aren't in charge of the growth. Stop doing the work for them and make them do it.

7 • START INVESTING

REFLECTION QUESTIONS

Answer these questions in a notebook to help you think about and apply the concepts in this chapter.

1. What is the end goal of your investment in the person you're helping?
2. Make a list of the ways you have enabled versus the ways you have invested.
3. How are you taking up your cross and following Jesus when helping the person in need?
4. How is your investment of instructions self-centered compared to Christ-centered?
5. How does your loved one respond to your investments?
6. Based on those responses, what do you need to change and what needs to stay the same?
7. What does obedience-based discipleship look like for the person you're helping?
8. Describe the atmosphere of change you're creating for your loved one.
9. Compare and contrast John's motivation when he was in the shelter and the person you are helping. What is different and what is the same?
10. From whom are you seeking godly counsel in order to invest wisely and not enable?

8
START BELIEVING
PEOPLE NEED PURPOSE

Matthew 4:19 (ESV)
And he said to them, "Follow me, and
I will make you fishers of men."

Jeremiah 29:11 (ESV)
For I know the plans I have for you, declares the Lord,
plans for welfare and not for evil, to give you a future and a hope.

What do these two verses have in common? I have one word for you: PURPOSE. Many people are looking for purpose in their lives and especially folks who come from addiction. *The Purpose Driven Life* by Rick Warren was on the New York Times Bestseller List for over 90 weeks. Over 32 million copies have been sold in more than 85 languages.[1] I believe the reason for

---
[1] https://en.wikipedia.org/wiki/The_Purpose_Driven_Life.

8 • START BELIEVING—PEOPLE NEED PURPOSE

Warren's success is the truth that people need purpose. I meet many people in this ministry and the thirst for purpose in life is very real.

I have said time and time again that people don't want to become Christians because Christians make Christianity look so boring. But throughout the New Testament you see Christ calling people for a purpose. Peter was made a fisher of men and Saul (who became Paul) was called to suffer while bearing the name of Jesus to the Gentiles, kings, and Jews (Acts 9:15). In the process of Paul's purpose, he planted many churches, won multitudes to Christ, and wrote thirteen books of the New Testament. Many times I look through the crowd at Freeway Ministries' North Campus, seeing the mass of hurting people and think, *These folks don't see that they have a purpose.* I know many who have bought into the lie that they will always be their mistakes. Honestly, even those who enable people stuck in addiction can hinder the addict with the things they say. See the "Breaking the Pattern" section at the end of this chapter for examples.

Just to be clear, **I don't believe a person has to stay a drug addict just because they've been in bondage to drugs. I refuse to place labels and stereotypes on people because they steal identity and purpose.** By being in the trenches serving with Freeway Ministries I have seen what purpose can do for a drug addict. **Drug addiction is a**

> LABELS & STEREOTYPES STEAL IDENTITY & PURPOSE

8 • START BELIEVING—PEOPLE NEED PURPOSE

master thief and one of the major things addiction steals from people is purpose.

Think about the things children talk about becoming when they grow up. I remember when my son, Keith,  was around five and we had one of our deep conversations. I said, "Keith, what do you want to be when you grow up?" We've had this talk repeatedly, but this time he said something I'll never forget. Keith looked at me as serious as he had ever been and said in his five-year-old voice, "Dad, when I grow up, I want to be a cowboy with a horse that won't throw me off." That boy had a dream with a purpose! What does this have to do with addiction? Keith had hope for a future with purpose. Have you ever asked a child, "What do you want to be when you grow up?" and they said, "A hopeless drug addict"? Have you ever heard a kid say, "When I grow up, I want to be a criminal and end up in prison"? Look what Jesus says about the enemy of our souls, Satan himself:

John 10:10 (ESV)
The thief comes only to steal and kill and destroy.
I came that they may have life and have it abundantly.

I share the truth of Scripture with folks who are spiritually bankrupt and totally destitute of hope. I look at them and deep down I know I see more potential in them than they see in themselves.

8 • START BELIEVING—PEOPLE NEED PURPOSE

When I'd been living in the homeless shelter for just a few weeks, I heard about a program that helped people re-enter society. I was so hungry to learn and get plugged into the community that I would've joined a women's basketball league if it would've helped. This program was grant-funded for those who signed up from prison. They had tons of resources but they weren't available to me because I just walked in from the street. The caseworker told me, "We don't have any funding for you because you didn't sign up from prison." They helped with nice clothing for job interviews, work boots, bus passes, some basic medical funding, and stuff like that. They also trained people to interview, do resumes, and they coached people through classes. I asked, "Can I stay without the benefits of the funding and learn what I can from you all?" They were shocked I still wanted to stay for the classes without the benefits of the clothing and medical funding, but I knew I had a purpose.

I remember telling my caseworker that God had called me to preach and start a ministry to help people like me come to know Christ, so they could have the same hope I had. He looked at me with a straight face and said, "Yes, that would be great if one day you can get involved with a church and maybe even lead a Bible study." Do you see what he did there? His opinion of my potential was not very high. He could have put my fire out. Today as I write this book, it's been nine years since having that conversation and I've never forgotten those words. Can you believe that? "Maybe even start a Bible study." He saw very little potential in my dreams. Don't put someone's fire out just because they're in active addiction. Sometimes hope is all a person has left. As long as they're still breathing, they can still fulfill their purpose.

> DON'T PUT AN ADDICT'S FIRE OUT—HOPE MAY BE ALL THEY HAVE LEFT

Does your counsel to the person who struggles with addiction include purpose? Share the truth of God's Word with them. Friend, your words have great potential. Ask them if they believe they have a purpose. Listen, we as Christians have what the secular world doesn't have, and that is hope. We have the hope of Scripture and the promises of God. Addicts oftentimes lose hope and purpose and they desperately need that hope back. Why do you think people do such stupid things while in active addiction? You're saying right now, "Because they're high on drugs or intoxicated." Yes, that's part of it, but there's much more behind it. Think about it for a minute. Addiction steals everything from a person. Every time they use, they care a little less about the things that used to mean the most to them—this is the slow fade. They stop caring about their health, finances, family, safety, and even their own freedom. People have unprotected sex with prostitutes, commit crimes knowing they are going to get caught, risk their lives, share needles with people they know may have a disease, and check out of their families. The addict has given up and feels as if they have no purpose left in life. They think they won't live much longer, so who cares if they use a dirty needle, catch a disease, or have a warrant out for their arrest. By this time in their addiction their family is an afterthought. They used to think they could be a mother or father, but now they're deep in addiction and any other purpose is something of the past. Many times addicts feel as if they would be doing their loved ones a favor if they would just die.

I would've taken my own life many times if I would've had the courage. I was so ashamed and defeated in my addiction. I felt like such a coward and knew I would be doing everyone a favor if I would disappear. I remember writing goodbye letters after doing so much cocaine and meth my heart seemed like it was going to explode. I remember sitting in a bathroom in a dirty trailer in the middle of nowhere weeping as I wrote an apology to the family I had left. I was sure I wouldn't make it through the day. I was in pain, lost, and felt like I had no reason to live another day.

Today I'm over ten years clean and sober and living every day to the fullest with purpose and hope. God has given me the opportunity to have two things I've always wanted: a Father and a life of purpose. I want to encourage you that your loved one can also have purpose in their life. They can change and I pray right now that you will believe that. Don't be like that caseworker who almost put my fire out. God can change the darkest heart regardless of where they are in life.

So what do we do with a person in that hopeless situation who's lost purpose? We need to share with them the very things they've lost: hope and purpose. You may think, *I don't know what to do. I've given the best advice I can, but nothing works.* One thing that never returns void is God's Word. Share the truth of the Bible with them. God's Word is full of hope and purpose for all people. God loves an underdog and my Bible is packed full of stories about underdogs who have triumphed. One of my favorite verses is 1 Corinthians 2:9 because in it I find purpose:  "Eye has not seen, nor ear heard, nor have entered into the heart of man the things which God has prepared for those who love Him" (NKJV). The purpose for God's people is beyond their imagination if they will just hold onto His Word and trust Him. When I preach at a church for the first time I say, "Drug addicts make some of the best Christians." The congregation usually looks at me like I have an extra eye on my forehead after saying that. Think about it for a minute. When someone who has lost all hope gets another chance at life, they're sold out. People who have been deep in the dark are very grateful for the light. I could write an entire book on what hope has done for this ex-junkie.

There's an overriding truth about sharing purpose with a person struggling with addiction: purpose changes and motivates people. I've memorized Bible stories about people who God changed with purpose. I know them by heart and can share them without a Bible in my hand. I am not telling you this to boast, but to challenge you to learn these stories for yourself. Let's say you're meeting with a loved one

8 • START BELIEVING—PEOPLE NEED PURPOSE

who's now homeless due to their addiction. They have been through everything you can imagine plus some. The bridges have been burned, they're desperate for some kind of hope, and you have a chance to share purpose with them. Where do you go from here? I have been in that situation and my favorite section of Scripture is Mark 5. This passage talks of a homeless man no one could tame, not even with chains. The world saw him as good as dead and that's why he was living in the tombs. He cried out day and night and never slept. He was a cutter and covered in scars. He was filthy, stinky, and unable to control his life. Society and even his friends had given up on him.

Does this sound like someone you know? Jesus went through a storm with His disciples to meet this man. Jesus cared for him when no one else did. He calmed him, clothed him, and put him in his right mind. Jesus also called this man into ministry. Not only did He not leave him like He found him, but He also gave him a purpose. I want you to imagine for a moment that you're standing on the shore with Jesus and this previously insane man. He's not a mad man anymore, but in his right mind. This guy was not only sane, but clothed. Think about it! This man was so far gone it was a shock he was dressed in public. The people who knew him from before were freaked out because of the radical change. The word Mark used to describe the reaction of those who knew this man was fear. They were afraid because he'd been transformed so dramatically.

When Jesus begins to leave, this once homeless, hopeless, naked, hurting, and purposeless man steps on the boat to follow Him. To his surprise, Jesus stops him. Jesus tells him that he has a purpose: "Go home to your friends and tell them how much the Lord has done for you, and how he has had mercy on you" (Mark 5:19, ESV). This man went from the town lunatic to the town preacher. Do you think he woke up that day and said, "I think I'll be delivered from these demons, get dressed, and be a preacher today"? I would argue against that. Jesus sought him out because He saw the purpose in a man everyone else saw as hopeless. I have shared that truth with homeless, hopeless, purposeless people and watched their countenance change instantly. These are not just stories, friend—they are powerful historical accounts found inside this wonderful book we study.

In Judges 6 we find a group of people who are desperate, hopeless, starved, and broke, without a plan or a place to call home. Have you ever studied the history of Israel during the time of the Judges? The Israelites were in a horrible position due to their rebellion against God. Does that sound familiar? These people who once walked with God are now starved and being bullied by the Midianites and Amalekites. They hid in the clefts of the rocks like bugs. Read for yourself in Judges 6:1-6. Gideon is called to deliver Israel from these oppressors while threshing wheat in the winepress to hide it from the Midianites. He is starved, hungry, and afraid of his own shadow, but God is pursuing him with a purpose. Place yourself there for a moment. The Angel of the Lord (who I believe was God Himself) shows up and He doesn't say, "Hey chicken, quit hiding and man up!" No, God says, "The Lord is with you, mighty man of valor" (see Judges 6:12). What do you think Gideon thought when God spoke to him in this way? I bet Gideon thought, *Mighty man of valor? I am hiding in a winepress afraid for my very life!* Then God says, "Go in this might of yours, and you shall save your people, Israel" (see Judges 6:14). Gideon thought God had abandoned and forsaken him, but that wasn't the case.

Let me make an application. Gideon needed purpose in his life. When God met him, he was suffering from direct rebellion against God and was homeless, hopeless, and without a purpose. Read that sentence again. Does that sound like someone you know? God called him a mighty man of valor because God didn't see Gideon as the man he *was*, but for the man he *could be*. The might of Gideon didn't have anything to do with his own strength, but God's promise and presence. God was with Gideon and promised to accomplish great things with his life. All Gideon had to do was believe, obey, and go.

> GOD DIDN'T SEE GIDEON FOR WHO HE *WAS*, BUT FOR WHO HE *COULD BE*

One of the things that often accompanies drug addiction is prostitution. I have met so many beautiful women made in the image of God who have fallen victim to prostitution because of their addiction. I have a story of purpose for the prostitute. I love sharing the story of the woman at the well with women who think God can't use a person who has been in prostitution. Stop and read the account of Jesus waiting for that woman in the heat of the day in John 4:1-42. Listen, Jesus was intentional and did something none of those religious people would've done: he asked for a drink from a Samaritan woman. This lady was in shock that a Jewish man would even speak to her, let alone ask her for a drink of water. Women drew water in the evening or early in the morning when it was cooler, but she was there in the heat of the day. She didn't want to see anyone and she didn't want anyone to see her either.

While the disciples were off getting a Happy Meal at McDonalds, Jesus had bread to eat that they didn't know about. That bread was to do the Father's will by reaching out to a woman riddled with shame and guilt. Jesus approached her and, according to her own testimony, told her everything she had ever done. He forgave her and gave her eternal life. The part of this story that is penetrating to the heart is that she'd had five husbands and was currently with another man who wasn't her husband. Jesus still reached out to her, saved her, used her, and gave her purpose. She was valuable to Jesus and He pursued her. What did this woman do when Christ saved her? She left her water bucket, ran to those people she was ashamed to face, and shared her testimony with boldness.

8 • START BELIEVING—PEOPLE NEED PURPOSE

Imagine for a moment you're right there on the edge of the village. You see the disciples come back with their Filet-O-Fish, but then you see this woman running to Jesus with a whole village of people. While you'd expect the disciples to be the ones to return with people to hear from Jesus, this woman was the one who came back with a harvest of souls. What changed with this woman? What made her leave her water and face those she was ashamed to see? Friend, <u>she met with Jesus, experienced forgiveness, and I believe, deep down, she found purpose.</u>

The means by which God moves is through His church. We as Christians are guilty of limiting God by our finite minds. We need these stories in our hearts and faith from God to believe that He can change a drug addict into a preacher. <u>Do you believe that God can change the worst of sinners? He already did with the apostle Paul! He did with you and me! The problem with your loved one is sin and a lack of hope. Share the hope of God's truth with them.</u> It doesn't cost you a thing!

8 • START BELIEVING—PEOPLE NEED PURPOSE

WORKING THROUGH THIS CHAPTER

IDENTIFYING THE PROBLEM

The person stuck in the cycle of addiction doesn't need to be told how much of an addict they are. There is a time to recognize that someone has a problem, but when they already know they're addicted, your loved one needs to see there is a purpose for their life and they can have another chance to live. They need hope! Don't listen to secular society's opinions and views of your loved one. Know that God can change a person and raise them up with a purpose. The world wants to stereotype the person struggling with addiction, but as a Christian we are called to find our identity in Christ, not our past or the sins we struggle with.

BREAKING THE PATTERN

Are you the person putting the fire out in someone's heart? Can I encourage you? Please don't give up on your loved one. You have to see that there is still a chance for them; not only to break free from their addiction, but to be more than a drug addict. I never introduce myself as, "Hello my name is John, and I'm an addict." I have an addictive personality, but I'm not an addict. I'm a child of God and that's where my identity is found.

Maybe you've unwittingly been discouraging your loved one. Here are some examples of how you may be hindering the addict with your words.

- Don't say things like, "You'll always be an addict because you have the disease of addiction" or "Addiction cannot be cured because it's a disease that can only be managed." These statements are very popular in secular recovery circles but very defeating. (Please read my paper, "The Sin of Addiction," in the Appendix for more information on the biblical vs. secular perspectives of addiction.)
- Avoid statements that give them an excuse to use like, "It's in your bloodline."
- Always avoid labels and talking down to them in any way.
- Avoid giving them the green light to play the victim. Don't allow them to blame others, their past, or their situation. The world is already giving them an excuse due to the disease model of addiction.
- I never like to use the word "can't" in a conversation with someone in addiction because, as my mother used to say, "Can't never could do nothing."

Conversely, here are some ideas for injecting hope into your loved one's life.

- Set down with your Bible and find stories of the underdogs God changed. Memorize one a week. Get sticky notes and put the Scripture where you can see it.

8 • START BELIEVING—PEOPLE NEED PURPOSE

Share those stories with your loved ones. Remember, these are historic encounters with Jesus, not just stories.
- Go to Freeway Ministries' YouTube channel and send them some testimonies of people who have been radically changed through Christ.
- Go to meetings with them. Even if your loved one won't go, it would do you some good to get involved in recovery-based meetings. You can learn from those in long-term recovery. We have many from different backgrounds who come to our weekly meetings. Many have never seen drugs but they have a burden for those in addiction. Whole families come to Freeway; mothers, fathers, children, and everyone loves the grandparents.
- Find someone who has a past like your loved one but is now living with purpose and have them share their testimony.
- Be a part of their recovery. Don't forget to encourage them, build them up, and remind them that God gives broken people purpose. They need you to believe they can change, so don't give up.
- Always look at addiction, criminal mentality, and other things that come from the culture of addiction from a biblical worldview. Let the Bible be the lens through which you look at every problem.

8 • START BELIEVING—PEOPLE NEED PURPOSE

▶ MOVING FORWARD

Make it a point to stop stereotyping from here on out. Begin to share hope and purpose regardless of how bad the situation may seem. Purpose drives a person, and discouragement puts on their brakes. Listen, God is still in the life-changing business. He is on the throne and He still delivers. No matter what, don't be the person to give up on someone, but instead share God's Word with them. Pray that God would reach deep into their hearts and change them through His Word with heavenly conviction.

8 • START BELIEVING—PEOPLE NEED PURPOSE

REFLECTION QUESTIONS

Answer these questions in a notebook to help you think about and apply the concepts in this chapter.

1. What purpose do you have when counseling an addict?
2. What is God's purpose for the addict?
3. How does your purpose line up with God's purpose?
4. What are you doing to encourage, build up, and give hope to the addict?
5. Memorize and explain 1 Corinthians 2:9.
6. How much time do you spend with God in prayer and study to understand your role in helping the addict find purpose?
7. Study Mark 5:1-20 and John 4:1-42. Identify Jesus' message and the sinners' response to Jesus.
8. What Bible passages and stories do you know that can give hope to the person you're helping?
9. How have you shared the hope in Christ with the person you love?
10. Thinking about your own life, who has given you hope when you were in sin?

9

IN CONCLUSION

I've been neck-deep in recovery ministry for several years now, having the privilege to do evangelism and outreach ministry, working with treatment centers, ministering at homeless shelters, and working with prisons and jails. Freeway Ministries' yearlong recovery program has reached two states and even Africa and is an alternative to prison in seven counties in Missouri. Our reputation speaks for itself. The lessons I've learned about enablement's role in addiction are all right here in this book. My prayer is that loved ones of those trapped in addiction would read it not only as a book, but as a resource. Use it in a small group setting, use it to encourage each other, and use it to help and not harm your loved one.

God gives people purposes, gifts, and certain burdens. I will never forget praying to God, "Use me like the drugs used me." I have spilled my heart out in this book to help

9 • IN CONCLUSION

you—this is who I am. I've learned that addiction causes more pain to the loved ones than it does the addict and they need help just as much as the person strung out on drugs. I pray that you will work through the chapters, identifying the problems of enablement, breaking those unhealthy patterns, and moving forward with your life as a parent or loved one of an addict. I pray this book will bring freedom to your life by giving you the tools to stop loving your kids to death.

# APPENDIX

APPENDIX

STOP COVERING FOR THEM TESTIMONY

Sarah's Story

What happened once you stopped covering for Hank?

Once I stopped covering, it was out! I now had tons of people praying for our situation who had no idea they needed to pray for us before as a direct result of me hiding "the secret." I now had help and support where pride had kept me from having any support or help for many years. I now had a plan of action that I never knew existed instead of just wondering what to do and trying to control it myself. I had searched high and low for secret help and support but I was isolated by both secrecy and my actual location. Once the secret was out, the ball was rolling and it was in the Lord's mighty and capable hands. I was FINALLY out of His way!

What did exposing him vs. covering for him do?

For about 13 years, I allowed Hank to have his cake and eat it too. I not only covered for him but I tried to go above and beyond as a wife. I foolishly thought I could somehow "love" him out of his addiction, so I did extra nice things for him and treated him with respect. I thought hiding his sin of addiction was somehow honoring his reputation.

He did not want his kids or anyone to know about his opioid or meth addictions. He would have been very angry if I had told anyone, so I spoke to no one about it. He didn't allow me to even talk to him about it. To be honest, I didn't want anyone to know! I was in complete denial about my own pride issues. But on a different level, I simply didn't want anyone to think badly of him. And so I enabled him to continue his addiction without any consequences. When you get in a habit for that many years of covert covering, it becomes automatic. It is always on your mind and you are always sick about it and always scared to death that someone is going to find out the truth. God has shown me something about all that: covering = lying. There, I said it. What it all boils down to is that I was a big, fat liar! I made excuses (lied) for him willingly because I had just as much at stake as he did if people ever found out. The thing that I hated the most and wanted gone from our lives was addiction and believe it or not, I had NO idea that my covering was allowing drugs to remain firmly planted in our lives. I did not know there was actually something I could do to get the ball rolling. I had done everything I knew to do—except tell the truth. I prayed. I begged God. I fasted. I spent years in tears, all the while acting like nothing was wrong when someone was around. I even acted like nothing was wrong around Hank, all the while my heart was falling out of my chest. We went to

APPENDIX

church 3x a week but no one knew because I hid it. I thought that exposure would ruin our lives! But it was a life that needed to be ruined for the chains of addiction to be broken.

When things got beyond unbearable, I fasted and prayed for wisdom. God showed me that wisdom without obedience was just advice (James 1:5-7). Before, my prayers were all, "Lord, please make him stop using." This time I prayed that God would show ME what to do and that He would give me the strength, courage, and grace to be obedient to do whatever He showed me. Three days after the fast, I got my answer and I didn't know that God would give me such clear direction, but here it was and I promised I would obey. I called John Stroup and he told me that the addict fears exposure the most. He told me to tell our kids and leave immediately. Within 30 minutes, I had a bag packed and was out the door and on the phone with my kids. It was by far the hardest thing I ever did. But harder days of resolve were coming! That simple act of obedience set the ball of freedom in motion... and what a motion it caused!! John put me in contact with a sweet lady who held me up in prayer and emotional support during this time. She was a wealth of play-by-play commentary on what would most likely happen next. She had seen it so many times. She was there to answer my questions as Hank fought tooth and nail to get me back and stay out of rehab! She advised me to not only quit answering texts and calls, but to block Hank from my phone. I couldn't imagine it! It all seemed so mean and cruel to me and I hated hurting him but I stuck to my obedience promise and did whatever she or John told me. They told me to stay hidden, to close access to bank accounts and cars and a host of other things that they knew were enablers at that time. It was all a big plan, taken from biblical examples, to get out of God's way and stop helping Hank to stay in his comfortable addiction. Finally, finally after several weeks and more prayer than I had ever prayed and less enabling than I had ever done, he reluctantly agreed to go to a Freeway men's house to get help before we could be back together as a couple. Far away with no money, no phone or car or any access to come back home, he BROKE! He gave his heart to Jesus! Praise be to God for His unspeakable gift! I can't even think about the "what ifs."

The struggles, the fears, the pain… This is the hardest part of these questions. The answers still bring me to tears.

The struggles: The struggle was, when I walked out of my house that day with a small bag of clothes and shut that door, I knew things were never going to be close to being the same ever again. We would never gather there together in that house with our family as we had for the past 27 years. Everyone in our small town would now look at me with pity or disdain. I was getting ready to break my children's hearts by telling them that their dad (who honestly had been such a good dad) was a drug addict—something they had no idea about.

APPENDIX

The fears: I was literally scared to death, shaking and crying. I feared what Hank might do when he found me gone. I was afraid he would force me to come back and nothing would change. I was afraid that he would kill himself and I voiced that fear to John. In fact, John told me on the phone before I left the house that he might do just that, but if he did, it would not be my fault. I almost buckled on this point alone! But he also told me that most addicts threatened suicide when their back was to the wall and most never went through with those threats. I feared the exposure! It is like digging up your most private and humiliating moment and then posting it on social media for everyone to see. I just had to overcome that fear, so I stepped out in obedience and faith and did not look back.

The pain: Well, I was already hurting so deeply that there are no words to truly describe how crushed my heart was by all the threats, lies, extreme anger, and manipulation that addition had caused. Truly, at this point, I was a broken woman held together by a faith in a strong and powerful God. I immersed myself in God's Word and Scripture songs by Esther Mui. God was my ROCK! But the pain that came after exposure and the subsequent action of leaving in order to begin the breaking process was just like a death. I thought so many times how similar the pain and emptiness were to the loneliness and separation of death. Having been married for over three decades and never being separated, my heart just ached for him and what he was going through. I wondered if we would ever be together again and it broke my heart. I thought that drugs had ruined our life together and let me tell you, that HURT!

What has God shown you through this?

Easiest answer! The #1 thing God has shown me is to hang my HOPE in one person only... Jesus Christ! Before, I had hope in Jesus as my Savior, but that was about it! I hoped Hank would change. I hoped I could do something to exact that change. I hoped nobody would have to find out. I hoped he wouldn't get caught or arrested. I hoped he would quit meth. Get the picture? Now, when I catch myself "hoping," I consciously flip that false hope and pray, "Lord, I put my hope in You alone." I learned that even if they don't mean to, people will always let you down because they are only human like me! But God will never let me down. He will never leave or forsake me and He is always for me! He has also shown me how unbelievably capable He is of changing a life! I have had a front row seat to see what the transforming power of the Holy Spirit inside of another person can do! It has really amped up my faith to know what God can do on a very, very personal level. Not like the Bible miracles we have read about since childhood, but in my own husband's life! This faith-building experience caused me to have a "God can do it" attitude. It has given me a true hope-filled expectation of seeing what God can and will do in any situation.

APPENDIX

What is your life and relationship like now?

Life is not all peaches and cream. It is hard because of the consequences of sin and bad choices. But I do have a new man now! One who is clean and sober, who will NOT steal a dime anymore, who won't lie to me, who doesn't get angry with me anymore, and who wouldn't say an unkind word to me! WOW! He reads his Bible every morning unprompted and won't listen to any worldly music. I don't have anything to cover up anymore! He does know I will not do that any longer.

Our relationship... It feels odd to trust him and for several months, I did not! For so long I was searching for stashes and never believing a word he said. So the major change is trust. The second is that I am not afraid because he no longer gets angry or tries to control me. Our lives are different in nearly every aspect. We lost a great deal, but God has been so good and has restored a lot of things and made them better!! We totally uprooted our lives and moved to get away from the environment and friends that Hank had. Again, this was at the wisdom of John and other godly counsel.

What would've happened if you continued enabling?

I honestly believe that Hank would not be alive today if things had continued at the pace and direction they were going. He would not have been saved and would have gone to hell because of the lies he had been telling himself. In order for something to change, something had to change and I

APPENDIX

thank God for John Stroup, Rick Lechner, and Freeway Ministries. Only God can reward you for all you do. I also thank my Father for giving me the grace I needed at such a desperate time in our lives.

APPENDIX

STOP CREATING A FALSE WORLD
TESTIMONY

A Success Story

"Real love rebukes and forgives." ~Paul Tripp

Love does not ignore wrong and hopes it goes away. Love may have to endure hardship and make sacrifices. I have learned through Freeway Ministries and my walk with the Lord that <u>when you know better you must do better.</u> I have seen God work miracles in the lives of broken people. True healing from the Lord comes when we pray for and allow a person to be broken. When we love someone it hurts to go through the broken phase with them, but that's what love does. Love endures.

    I remember sitting down at the family dinner table. My parents were both retired, living in a very nice home on the outskirts of Springfield. We sat at this table to eat lunch almost every Sunday after church. But now, sitting down at this table wasn't for fellowship and enjoying dinner together. We began sitting down at this table often, having discussions that were very heated, very complicated, and more times than not, led to discouragement and sorrow. My mom, then at the

APPENDIX

age of 62 years old, had gotten out of control using methamphetamine. Because I love my mom I had to take a very hard stand. Because I love my mom I could not sweep this issue under the rug hoping it would just go away. Much like a cancer, when sin issues are left unchecked, they will infect and take over a person's entire life.

Peeling layers back to get to the truth takes patience and consistency. I couldn't tell you the countless hours spent sitting down at that table, uncovering lies that my mom couldn't keep straight. I remember being called a self-righteous, judgmental know-it-all. I also remember getting kicked out of my mom's house. But I kept going back. One thing she could count on was that I was not going to make it easy for her to live the lifestyle of her choice. Freeway Ministries is considered a "full contact" ministry and that is exactly how I went about it. I got in her business even when it wasn't welcomed.

I don't know how many people have ever dropped a drug test on their own mom, but I did. Twice. She failed miserably each time. The first time failing the test she said it was the "cold medicine's" fault, the second time it was clearly a "defective test". She had answers and excuses for everything. But the drug test didn't lie. Now that we had evidence of her drug use we could move forward with the issue. The drug test results were a hard fact for my dad. There was now a reality that he had to face.

APPENDIX

One of the biggest blessings at this time was the family unit that formed during this hardship. God strengthened us for this fight and equipped us to go through everything we were going to go through. My loving wife, who pulls no punches with the truth, was right there beside me the entire time. My teenage son, heartbroken by the fact his grandmother was using drugs, did his best to be encouraging through it all. My dad was scared and uncertain of what life was going to hold for him and my mom. Truthfully, we were all heartbroken and scared. Fortunately, in brokenness and fear is when the Lord works the best.

We had identified the problem; the obstacle for me was how in the world do you deal out consequences to your mom? I spent a lot of time seeking wise counsel. I knew I needed help. I spent a lot of time in prayer. Had I not asked for help, I probably would have done things in my own strength and would have been making emotional and unwise decisions based on feelings. Taking the personal sting out of the situation was the hardest part. I had to realize my mom's rebellion wasn't against me, it was against the Lord. Her problem wasn't just the drugs, it was sin. I wanted my mom to be free from her addiction to meth, but more importantly I wanted her to be reconciled and in right standing with the Lord. I would like to say my attitude towards her got better after realizing the situation she was truly in, but the fact was, I was hurt. I was angry. I had grown tired of it all, but I didn't quit. Love is patient. Love endures.

APPENDIX

My mom agreed to go to a drug treatment center in Alabama—a 90-day treatment center, almost twelve hours away. Summer had just started and life as we knew it was about to get turned upside down. My family was about to make some serious sacrifices and get extremely uncomfortable, to say the least. Had life been normal aside from this, it may have been a little easier. However, my mother-in-law was battling stage four cancer and we had to juggle schedules and make a lot of road trips to care for her on the weekends. Love sacrifices.

I remember dropping my mom off at the treatment center. I couldn't leave fast enough, but driving away from her gave me the same feeling I felt as a young man leaving the prison after visiting my dad. It hurt. I believed it was necessary though. My mom completed the program. I got to pick her up and attend her graduation that day. I would like to say everything was magically better, but it wasn't. I was still hurt. She was sober, she was better, she had time to process things, but sin has consequences. A consequence of my mother's sin was the relationship she and I once had was destroyed. A twelve-hour car ride is a very long time. The conversations got heated once again, there was a lot of quiet time, and I remember when dropping my parents off at their home my mother and I literally were throwing her luggage and other belongings out of the van in the driveway. I left angry, hurt and felt very defeated. What just happened? I had to take some time to cool down. After all this time, effort and energy, things were still a mess and I was still a mess. But, love endures. I had to take necessary steps to show my mom the same mercy and grace that Jesus showed me. It wasn't easy. It wasn't natural, but it was necessary. Love forgives. The word forgive takes on the meaning of "let it go." That has been a process for me, not a one-time moment.

Reflecting on this time in my life I can honestly say it was hard work, but it was worth it. It would have been easy to ignore the wrong in my mom's life. It would have been easier on my family and me to have ignored the problem in hopes of it just going away. We could have stayed silent and been passive about all the issues. Perhaps she would have eventually straightened up, but she also could have ended up dead.

Instead, my mom has repented of her sin and has received Jesus as her Lord and Savior. My mom now sings in the church choir and also serves alongside women who have been or are currently going through the same things she has. She uses her life experiences to help other women. My mom reads her Bible daily, seeking wisdom and help from the Lord. My mom rides on the church vans helping my dad pick people up and get them to church. I have watched my parent's relationship build and become stronger, where most people would have just given up. Through the trials of her addiction, the Lord has shown both my mom and me that the relationship we once thought was solid was not at all how the He wanted it to be. Through the pain she and I have a new relationship, one built on the solid foundation of the Lord, and that relationship is better than ever before. Denial of this

APPENDIX

issue would have been the easy way out. Pretending things weren't the way they truly were would have never allowed us to see the fruit of following God's plan in our lives.

APPENDIX

GENERATIONAL ADDICTION & ENABLEMENT TESTIMONY

There have been three generations of addicts/abusers before me that I know of. From what I can tell, enablement goes back at least that far. Makes sense, right? They go hand in hand. Generational enablement brings an added level of complexity to the bondage. There seems to be no escape. The newest generation is tossed from parent to grandparent to great grandparent, each trying to fix what the other failed to fix in their own broken way, with each new effort only strengthening the stronghold.

My father died before I turned one year old. He was talented but abusive and very unstable. His father died when my dad was a young adult. Both deaths were a result of drug addiction. One suicide, the other driving while under the influence. Both left behind a broken family that had no true means of coping with the tragedies. So, we all continued in the example set before us: addiction.

I remember discussing our family history at an early age and feeling very entitled. People were brokenhearted and often did anything in their power to assist me. There were two problems with this approach. First, I didn't even know what type of assistance I needed. Second, <u>I had to remain a victim to continue to receive this type of help. It's hard to be an overcomer when being a victim is so accepted and profitable.</u>

Even when I began to understand that my method of dealing with life was unhealthy, I would always get drawn back into it. It was a short cycle to dealing with life's issues. Short in that I didn't continue through the tough challenges to mature me beyond my current situation. Short in that it only took about one year to go from bottom to a hopeful new beginning back to bottom again. So, what changed this cycle in my life? When the cycle was interrupted.

I was sitting in a jail cell with a Class A felony of manufacturing methamphetamine where children reside. I was looking at a lot of time behind bars. This was not a new situation for me. This was part of my cycle. It was the place where I usually made promises to my family, to myself, and to God. The place where they would convince themselves to believe me and take me back into their home to help me start the cycle over again. <u>The difference this time was that I knew I could never keep those promises. I was a liar and I was sick of hearing my own lies.</u> I knew deep inside that I didn't even have the power to carry out the lies that I always promised in order to rally support and bargain for a better deal. For the first time in my life I didn't try to convince others that I was going to change. This is the first time I didn't attempt to make deals with God to get me out of the situation. What I did was simply hang my head and cry. <u>I was hopeless. I was helpless.</u>

APPENDIX

God was moving in ways that I couldn't have known. He was working through the sheriff's department in apprehending me. They put me in a situation I couldn't escape. God was working though my family. My kids didn't even want to talk to me on the phone. They were tired of being taken advantage of and being taken for granted. God was moving in the people he was sending into the jail to minister to me.

Each person God sent into the jail said something that penetrated my mind and heart. One young man's testimony, in a simplified form, described my life. This young man stole something from his neighbor's house then ran home and hid in shame and guilt. That young man then repented to a holy God. This was my story. I have spent my whole life running and hiding in shame and guilt. Then God spoke to me though a pastor who was totally convinced the Bible was the Word of God and it was the only Truth we could trust. Then God spoke through a street evangelist who had once gone to the darkest, nastiest places to continue in his drug addiction. Now he went to similar dark places to be a light with the hope he found in Christ Jesus. God was moving in all these ways, but something happened when I opened the Bible one of these men handed me.

I had read the Bible before, but this time it was different. I knew that this was not just another truth or an alternative to my will. This was the only thing that could help me. I began to read it as though it was more real than my feelings, more real than what others said. In a place where there should have been nothing but fear, uncertainty, and regret, I began to have hope. At first, I cried tears of sorrow as I began to understand that the things I've done with my life weren't just against myself and others but against a holy God. Then I began to cry tears of joy as I understood that despite all the things I have done against Christ, He still loved me. This is the first time in my life I didn't feel like I had to reach some level of performance to be accepted and loved.

My mind and heart began to soften to these truths. Then one day I read a verse that crushed me entirely. Matthew 12:30: "If you don't gather with Me, you scatter abroad, he who is not with Me is against Me." I could no longer deal with myself. Everything I had done in my life was pushing others away from Him. That was more than I could bear. Knowing I didn't bring much to the table, really nothing at all, I surrendered all of me with whatever was left of this life. I made the decision to be found each day following in His presence as I studied His Word. I also knew that in order to walk this out on the other side of those concrete walls I had to surround myself with people who were already living this out in their lives. I had no idea where that was; I only knew I could not go home again.

Going home was always a fresh start to the cycle that spiraled down to a new, lower bottom each time. I was scared to try to start over on my own. I was scared of moving somewhere new where I didn't know anyone. I was scared I would have to let others know what a mess I was and that I

APPENDIX

needed help. But I refused to go back to the comforts of home where I would be forced to live a compromised Christianity. I had to do all of those scary things as I now began to learn the process of "dying to self."

When I started fresh, is was in a place I've never been, Springfield, Missouri. I home planned to a halfway house that was supposed to be faith-based, but I quickly began to see many of the compromises being displayed that I was attempting to flee. I was discouraged and felt that old cycle beginning to creep up again. But I continued in the Bible and continued to pray, and God was faithful. Freeway Ministries began to pick me up for their meetings. For the first time in my life I was introduced to a group of men from my background living out the life that I had attempted so many times. They were no longer defined by the events of their past but had been matured by them. They were not victims but overcomers. And they began to pour into me the difficult lessons necessary for me to overcome.

For the first time in my life I began to grow and stand on my own two feet. My family felt like I was rejecting them, but I was taking responsibility for my actions and making amends for what I had done in the past. I was maturing and miracles were happening. I held a job for more than six months, had my own apartment, and paid the bills. I became engaged to a godly woman, honored the engagement until we were married, and we purchased a home together. Miracles only God could do. Miracles we grew through. Then came the day that we had the opportunity to move my daughters from my first marriage into our home.

This was an opportunity our church had joined us in prayer about for several years. It's also one of the biggest messes we've gotten mixed up in during our Christian walk. Now comes the fourth generation of addicts/abusers/enabled sinners. We were so quick to praise God for the opportunity of letting us parent those two girls. This was the first time they experienced consistent accountability and consequences. They didn't respond well. And sadly, their escape plan was only a phone call away. The same family that taught me I didn't have to face the consequences of my selfish decisions was now teaching it to my daughters. So, they allowed the girls to move back into their home and out of the responsibility of dealing with life on life's terms. It broke our hearts, but God showed us we had an opportunity we didn't deserve. We were given the chance to pour the best of what God had given us and what the church had taught us into these girls who needed it. We praised Him with tears running down our face.

It wasn't long before they hit another bottom in their cycle. As with so many in my family, the compromise in God's plan comes with a return to bondage to co-dependent relationships as well as drug and alcohol dependency. So the quick fix of running from discipline to a place of ease and comfort fell apart again. The girls called us asking for help. My parents also called stating they didn't know what to do

APPENDIX

with these crazy girls. This time we set boundaries and everyone agreed that when the newness of the fresh start wore off, the girls would remain with us to grow through the pangs of maturity. I honestly thought we were on the same page. Again, with the help of the church we poured our lives into these two. They were growing and bringing areas of their lives into obedience. Prayers were being answered. They were serving in the church and developing relationships with other Christians. It was a great time in our lives. Then again during a time of uncomfortable growth they called the people who always seemed to make their problems go away: my parents. And again, we were left with a gaping hole in our heart. Yet, we praised God.

This time we began to understand that we were not simply taking our kids in and then turning them back over to the world. We were trusting God with them through the whole process. We were placing these girls in God's hands whether they were part of our home or whether they were just part of our prayer requests. It was the same faithful God who was moving in their lives to accomplish what we could not, helping them to see for themselves how empty this world and its help is.

They were once again stuck in that cycle where they had to play the victim; that old familiar place where they were not allowed to grow or take responsibility. They could only agree with the terms of the help they were receiving and that meant that they had to be dependent on the help my parents offered them. This sadly was the reward my family got out of

APPENDIX

this unhealthy condition—they got to feel like they were fixing the broken kids. In reality they were preventing needed healing and growth from happening. My kids needed to turn their backs on the world's help and reach for Christ alone, then the church would be what it is intended to be in their lives: a family.

Unfortunately, that is where this story leaves off, at least for one of our daughters. For the other, she has made up her mind that she is not accepting a worldly solution to her spiritual problem, and we pray that she continues. Today she is beginning her day in her Bible. It is a condition for living in our home. She is also participating in church and ministry activities. It is a condition of her spiritual wellbeing. But most importantly, she is not bound to the someone else's opinion of her worth. She is drawing near to a God who tells her her worth in His Word. And praise God, she is raising her children not only in church, but through her example of pressing on through this life's trials.

APPENDIX

The Sin of Addiction:
Seeing Addiction as Sin and the Road to Recovery

John Stroup

EN 1102—Composition II Fall 2015 (Online)

December 5, 2015

APPENDIX

I once read a story about a man who lost his keys and searched in the street for hours until the sun went down. Later, his friends came over to help him continue the search. For hours into the night, they helped him search. They looked in the front yard, the back yard, under the porch.

Then one of his friends asked him, "Where did you last see your keys?"

"Inside the house," the man replied.

The same story holds, I would argue, for the key to addiction recovery. Our nation is looking for this key in all the wrong places. Crime, abuse, child neglect, disease, and many other social ills are due to addiction. Drug and alcohol abuse are tearing America apart, and people are looking for an answer. In 2015, the federal government spent 26.3 billion dollars in drug prevention and control, and the "president has requested 27.6 billion for 2016"[1] as the problem worsens. In this paper, I will argue that the key to addiction recovery *can* be found—if we learn to look for it in the right place. The key will not be found in medicine, for the root of the problem is not medical. Further, the craving to use drugs may be powerful, but it is not uncontrollable. While most treatment programs today treat addiction as a disease, the Bible tells us clearly that addiction is sin, and that the root of addiction, *as sin*, is selfishness; so we must look to the Bible for answers to drug addiction and alcoholism.

---

[1] "National Drug Control Budget." www.whithouse.gov. February 1, 2015. Accessed November 12, 2015. https://www.whitehouse.gov///sites/default/files/ondcp/press-releases/ondcp_fy16_budget_highlights.pdf.

APPENDIX

My life is invested in the subject of this paper. While working with addiction, and being in recovery, my life's work is helping people recover from addiction, criminality, and the bad lifestyle choices that result from or lead to an addiction lifestyle. The purpose of this paper is to explore the root cause of addiction, examine the secular disease model, and argue that the biblical understanding of addiction as sin gives real hope for recovery.

Exploring the Root Cause

According to the Institute of Medicine, the American Psychiatric Association, and the American Medical Association, addiction is as an uncontrollable, compulsive craving, seeking, and use of drugs, regardless of consequences.[2] This is an accurate description of addictive behavior, but not of the root of addiction, as Alan Leshner puts it in his article, "Addiction is a Brain Disease."[3] Who would argue against the fact that controlling an addict's cravings is the main concern? We can all agree about the behaviors tied to addiction. But agreement on the root of addiction is another story altogether. Addicts live in the midst of cravings. But we do not look for the roots of *anything* in the middle—instead, we look for roots at the beginning, where things start. Addiction begins *before* cravings, and results from needs that have not been met. And these needs are

---

[2] Leshner, Alan. "Addiction Is a Brain Disease." *Issues in Science and Technology* 17.3 (Spring 2001): 2. Accessed October 29, 2015. Professional Development Collection.
[3] Ibid.

spiritual. When someone has no belief in the supernatural, then, as the Bible tells us, he cannot understand issues of the heart (see 1 Cor 2:6-10). And the heart is where the problem lies (Jer 17:9). The root of addiction is sin according to the Bible, and the root of all sin comes from self (see Jam 1:13-15). Sin comes from the fall of man in the Garden of Eden, when man placed pleasing self over pleasing God. If we look into any addiction through the Bible, we will see that the root is the selfishness of sin. The further people go into using drugs, the less they care about consequences, others, and even their own health. The number one drive of addiction is pleasure, lust, and trying to fill a void within self. It is a void that has been carved into us through sin. And it is a void that can be filled only by God through His Son, Jesus Christ.

Alan Leshner is a prominent spokesperson for the disease model of addiction, so I shall use him to focus my arguments. According to Leschner, there is no way to tell where the line is drawn between uncontrollable drug use and that place where one becomes clinically addicted. So how can the root—which, according to Leshner is "the only thing that should matter"[4]—be an uncontrollable craving? The secular treatment doctors who view addiction as a disease admit that they cannot determine when functional or controllable use becomes an addiction. So how can they say that the root of addiction is an uncontrollable craving? That does not make sense, due to the fact that someone is already using drugs

---

[4] Ibid.

APPENDIX

before they cross the line from uncontrollable drug cravings to becoming clinically addicted. Would it not make more sense to explore what drives someone to use a drug, or indulge in alcohol in the first place? Wouldn't it make more sense to search out the issues a person has when they began to use a substance? Again, when exploring the root of something one starts at the beginning, or explores where something came from. When a person deals with addicts on a daily basis through an effective recovery ministry, it becomes obvious that the problem is the heart, and the foundation of the addict's identity has a major impact on that person's need to use.

As Christopher Cook notes in his book, *Alcohol, Addiction and Christian Ethics*, "prior to the nineteenth century drunkenness was always considered a sin by all Christians."[5] Nowadays, this view has lost its popularity, due to secular psychology. The Bible is clear that the root of man's sin nature derives from the fall of man in the Garden of Eden, and that addiction is a type of sin. Secular psychologists, however, reject sin, the Bible, and the role of the Spirit in addiction and recovery. They would treat the addict by means of behavioral therapy and, most commonly, by medication.[6] In an article concerning lifestyle balance, Glyn Davies makes it clear that people turn to drugs as a "coping mechanism."[7] Drug use is a

---

[5] Ibid.
[6] Leshner.
[7] Davies, Glyn, et al. "The Role of Lifestyle in Perpetuating Substance Use Disorder: the Lifestyle Balance Model." *Substance Abuse Treatment, Prevention & Policy* 10.1 (June 2015): 1-8. Academic Search Complete, EBSCOhost, accessed December 2, 2015.

symptom of deeper life issues: the addict's failure to find happiness in life drives him or her to substance abuse. A biblical understanding makes it clear that our sin nature is the deep underlying cause of addictive behavior, and that addicts turn to drugs as a means to cope. Ask scientists to describe addiction and its cause, and they will agree that it is a "brain disease," though they cannot agree on what causes a person to start using a substance that leads to clinical addiction.[8] Some will say it is genetics. Others will say that it is neurobiological. Others will say that it is social-cognitive—or learned, or behavioral, or cultural, or psychological in origin.[9]

The Disease Model of Addiction

Those who embrace the disease model do have a valid point regarding the neurological and physical *consequences* of addiction. After all, brain tests show the considerable damage from effects of continued substance abuse. There is not a person from either side that would deny the effects that drugs and alcohol have on the brain. For many, therefore, the physiological effects of addiction give proof supporting the brain disease model. As Leshner writes, there are only "two ways to view addiction,"[10] *and sin is not one of them*. To say that there are only two ways to look at addiction recovery is a big fallacy. There is huge success in faith-based treatment programs that don't involve the two ways Leshner mentions.

---

[8] Ibid.
[9] Ibid.
[10] Leshner.

APPENDIX

Among these faith-based programs, I would mention Celebrate Recovery, Reformers Unanimous, Addicts Victorious, Teen Challenge, and Freeway Ministries just to name a few.

When people hear of someone having a disease, the last thing they think about is addiction. They may think of cancer, AIDS, asthma, or some other illness that has infected a person's life. According to Carla Meurk of BMC Psychiatry,[11] the view of the secular treatment world at large is that addiction is a disease, like diabetes or hypertension.[12] The well-known group Alcoholics Anonymous holds onto the disease model of addiction. According to Nicholas Boeving, in the year of 2000 93% of secular treatment centers used Alcoholics Anonymous as part of their treatment for addiction.[13] An assumption of these treatment centers is that the addict cannot ever be cured but only remain in remission through meetings, and medication. The idea behind this view, in a nutshell, is that "there is no cure"[14] for the drug user.

Understanding addiction from personal experience, I cringe at this viewpoint due to the hopelessness it brings. Though Alcoholic Anonymous is a great place to cope, and many begin their journey toward recovery there, the success rate is very discouraging. It seems that only 5% recover

---

[11] Meurk.
[12] McLellan, A. Thomas, et al. "Can Substance Use Disorders be Managed Using the Chronic Care Model? Review and Recommendations from a NIDA Consensus Group." *Public Health Reviews* 35.2 (January 2014): 2107-6952.
[13] Boeving, Nicholas G. "Sneaking God (Back) Through the Back Door of Science: A Call for a Comparative Addictionology." *Pastoral Psychology* 59 (2009): 93-107.
[14] Ibid.

APPENDIX

successfully through the philosophy of this group. A study was done to see the percentage of alcoholics who had made improvement to the point of remission from drinking, and the results speak for themselves. Following up with fifty-eight people who struggle with drinking, 15% remained abstinent after one year, and 11% were abstinent after three years.[15] Now here is the catch to this study: these fifty-eight people had no treatment for their drinking. Now compare that to the 5% of those whose addiction was treated through the disease model and its methods. Something is obviously missing in this aspect of addiction recovery.

I argue that people choose to drink or do drugs. Yet the thought of *choosing a disease* sounds ridiculous to anyone. How many people make a choice to have diabetes or hypertension? Today, addiction is seen by the majority of treatment centers as a disease, and yet the treatment is not making a noticeable impact in recovery. Before the nineteenth century, addiction was sin, and all the medical labels and diagnosed disorders were not prevalent as they are today. For every so-called addiction today, the Bible speaks on the subject and makes it clear that it is sin. What was once called gluttony is now being called pathological overeating. What the Bible calls a thief today is called a kleptomaniac. Someone the Bible describes as full of greed today would be labeled as suffering from the disorder of consumerism.

---

[15] Boeving, Nicholas G.

APPENDIX

The theories of secular psychiatry, psychology, and those who practice the disease model come from the *Diagnostic and Statistical Manual of Mental Disorders* or the D.S.M. This book is supposed to hold the answers to man's struggles and disorders. The Bible is disregarded, along with the God of the Bible, and is replaced with the D.S.M. The argument that the secular world at large is making comes down to the worldview that there is no God and no supernatural. The atheistic view is that man is an evolved animal, so the problem must be biochemical. The atheist denies that man has a soul or spirit, so addiction must be biological. The issue has to be dealt with on a biological level, and that means treatment through chemicals. I will discuss this in more detail a little further on, but one thing must be looked at before then.

The D.S.M., which the secular treatment world turns to for diagnosis, is largely supported by pharmaceutical companies. Look what Rachel Cooper has to say about the connection between pharmaceutical companies and those who write and revise the D.S.M. When the D.S.M. comes up with new symptoms, now "there is a market for new drugs."[16] The American Psychiatric Association receives millions of dollars every year from the companies that make drugs to advertise their products. This mindset rewards men for coming up with chemical answers to addiction recovery. That

---

[16] Cooper, Rachel. *Diagnosing the Diagnostic and Statistical Manual of Mental Disorders.* London: Karnac Books, 2014. EBSCOhost ebook, accessed December 1, 2015.

answer is more drugs, more labels, more disorders, and more excuses for relapse.

The Road to Recovery through the Disease Model

How does a person overcome in battling addiction, one may ask? Those who view addiction as a disease have several answers to that question, and their diagnosis will come from their authoritative book, the D.S.M. Those who view addiction as a sin will find their answer a Book called the Bible—a Christian's manual for healing. Those who embrace the disease model call the sin model "erroneous, and simple,"[17] claiming further that addiction, as a chronic illness, cannot be cured but only managed. Those who embrace the sin model would say that everyone has sin in their lives and that sin takes many forms—addiction being just one of them.

The disease model sees a road to recovery that is paved with a life of battling a disease that will never be cured. It is a lifetime of medication and support meetings. Treatment programs based in Alcoholics Anonymous claim that you can make a higher power of your own understanding. This higher power can be anything you want to put your faith in. One counselor said his higher power was the ocean, because "as a surfer he knew the ocean was more powerful than him."[18] They pray to this higher power and surrender to their higher power. The Christian would agree that faith is vital, that

---

[17] Leshner.
[18] "The God Thing." *Addict Science* . Web. November 11, 2011. Accessed December 3, 2015. http://www.addictscience.com/the-god-thing/.

APPENDIX

surrender is vital, and prayer is vital as well. But the foundation of one's faith and the direction of prayer is what is in question. The disease model has an answer for cravings, and desire for relapse, as Alan Leshner puts it, "can easily be managed with proper medications."[19] The D.S.M. will look at the symptoms and diagnose the person struggling with addiction with medication to handle the biological effects from addiction.

While I agree that a person might need medication in certain circumstances (for example, when showing severe withdrawal symptoms), there is a serious danger to this. The leading medication today in addiction recovery is Methadone or Burprenorphine. This medication is the biomedical field's answer for relapse prevention. But Methadone is deadly. According to the Pew Trust research, "Methadone overdoses kill about 5,000 people every year, six times as many as in the late 1990s, when it was prescribed almost exclusively for use in hospitals."[20] Methadone is also known to be a "highly addictive drug."[21] While we can be thankful for the wonders of medicine, one has to question why the answer to addiction must be something deadly and addictive? By looking at addiction as a chronic disease and treating it chemically, there is one more danger to recovery from addiction. The chronic disease becomes a green light to blame addiction on

---

[19] Leshner.
[20] Vestal, Christine. "Most States List Deadly Methadone as a 'Preferred Drug.'" Web. April 1, 2015. Accessed December 3, 2015. http://www.pewtrusts.org/en/research-and-analysis/blogs/stateline/2015/4/23/most-states-list-deadly-methadone-as-a-preferred-drug.
[21] Ibid.

something besides the drug user. After all, how can you hold someone accountable for shaking who has Parkinson's disease? When drug addiction is lined up besides Parkinson's disease, cancer, and hypertension, there is a way to justify using drugs. And what about disability? The American Disability Act sees addiction as a disability.[22] That leaves employers who refuse to hire addicts due to drug-driven crime in danger of lawsuits. How do you feel about someone filing for a disability due to addiction and collecting a check?

The Road to Recovery Treating Addiction as Sin
Seeing addiction as sin is biblical. The manual that the Christian uses, unlike the D.S.M., never has to be updated and has diagnoses for man's life issues. Unfortunately, the Bible has been watered down and its concepts have been stolen to suit a humanistic society. Like the secular treatment's view of addiction, sin cannot be cured, but it has been dealt with on the cross. The only way an addict can break free from addiction is a spiritual surrender similar to the twelve-step idea of Alcoholics Anonymous. The Christian also prays for power, but that power comes in the form of the God of the Bible. The first thing that someone who is suffering from the bondage of any sin needs is to hear the Word of God, because that is where faith comes from (see Rom 10:9-13). Then they need to surrender to the Lord Jesus Christ. According to the Bible, He is the only higher power. So salvation is a must.

---

[22] Westreich, Laurence M. "Addiction and the Americans with Disabilities Act." *Journal of the American Academy of Psychiatry and the Law Online* 30.3 (2002): 355-363.

APPENDIX

The second step towards recovery is community. The person struggling with addiction needs an environment full of people who can support them through their struggles. That environment is called the church. According to the Substance Abuse Treatment Prevention policy, "social networks an individual belong to also play a major role in determining what kind of lifestyle they lead."[23] This is a biblical concept that teaches one to watch who one associates with, and that the wrong crowd will have a corrupting impact on one's life (1 Cor 15:33). When someone takes a step away from a drug addict or criminal and then becomes a part of the church, it changes that person. The programs that secular recovery use call it service work, but the Bible calls it serving the Lord. People with addictions find their purpose in the church, and then have that new community of fellowship they need. As Warren Wiersbe writes, "nature depicts appetite, and environment."[24]

The last step is becoming a fully obedient follower of Jesus Christ. This is where the people learn who they are in Christ, and studying the Bible gives them power. They learn how to deal with their sin by placing faith in the only perfect manual—the Bible. Working with other believers in Christ who have been through those struggles, and having others invest in them is a major step towards recovering. Seeing themselves as sons of God and not as addicts gives them hope

---

[23] Glyn Davies.
[24] Wiersbe, Warren W. *The Wiersbe Bible Commentary: The Complete New Testament in One Volume*. 2nd ed. Colorado Springs, CO: David C. Cook, 2007.

for a future. Learning that God is not a respecter of persons and that they can be more than addicts is motivation to continue on the road to recovery. Having a chance to start over again with a new life in Christ spells hope, and that is a huge motivator. I heard a man say, "I still get high today, but today I get high off helping people change their lives."

Conclusion
In closing, there are many ways to fight the battle of addiction, and there are many different answers that one may gather to define addiction. Seeing oneself as an addict for the rest of one's life, with a disease that cannot be cured, is depressing. Replacing a street drug that is highly addictive and deadly with a prescription drug that is also highly addictive and deadly doesn't cut it either. This makes as much sense as someone who has won a battle with overeating and is maintaining a healthy lifestyle going to a meeting and calling themselves obese every day. Seeing addiction as a sin like any other sin is freeing and makes much more sense. Yes, sin is always going to have an effect on man until Jesus redeems man and then the believer will be perfect. Looking through the Bible, one has hope, and less discrimination. Instead of introducing themselves as addicts, they can introduce themselves as children of the King. People join a new community where they are held accountable, can work, and become useful with a purpose. They learn from the manual Christians use called the Bible. They begin learning

APPENDIX

principles and disciplines for life. They stay out of prison, start paying taxes, and stop breaking the law. What an impact this makes on the community and the economy as a whole. According to the *Federal Register*, "The fee to cover the average cost of incarceration for Federal inmates in Fiscal Year 2014 was $30,619.85 ($83.89 per day)."[25] Just think of the difference that can be made by keeping ex-addicts out of jail.

Think about what success looks like from the two views of addiction recovery. The disease model would say that sobriety is success, while the sin model would say that following Christ is success. A person can commit crime, live immorally, and do terrible things while one is sober. A true follower of Christ lives with the desire to please their God out of love for Him, and does his best to walk in the light. Seeing addiction as sin gives a person freedom, purpose, hope, and a way to be more than an addict.

---

[25] "Dodd-Frank Wall Street Reform 277." *Federal Register*. Accessed December 1, 2015. https://www.federalregister.gov/articles/2015/03/09/2015-05437/annual-determination-of-average-cost-of-incarceration.

JOHN STROUP

John enjoys preaching, planting ministries, high school assemblies, and ministering to a wide range of organizations about overcoming odds through Christ. If you are interested in John for your event, use the contact info below.

PHONE	MAILING ADDRESS	WEBSITES
(417) 616-1941	Freeway Ministries PO BOX 8655 Springfield, MO 65801	freeway-ministries.com johnstroup.net

Freeway Ministries depends on the generosity of God's people. If you would like to support Freeway Ministries, contact John today.

Made in the USA
Lexington, KY
20 September 2019